A sect that moved the world : three generations of Clapham saints and philanthropists – Primary Source Edition

John Telford

A SECT THAT MOVED
THE WORLD

A SECT THAT MOVED THE WORLD

*THREE GENERATIONS OF CLAPHAM
SAINTS AND PHILANTHROPISTS*

BY

JOHN TELFORD, B.A.

AUTHOR OF
'THE LIFE OF JOHN WESLEY,' 'THE LIFE OF CHARLES WESLEY,'
'THE STORY OF THE UPPER ROOM,' 'WESLEY'S CHAPEL AND
WESLEY'S HOUSE,' ETC.

WITH PORTRAITS AND ILLUSTRATIONS

London
CHARLES H. KELLY
2 CASTLE STREET, CITY ROAD, AND 26 PATERNOSTER ROW, E.C.

PRINTED BY
HAZELL, WATSON AND VINEY, LD.,
LONDON AND AYLESBURY.

Dedicated

TO

PERCY M. THORNTON, Esq., M.P.,

OF BATTERSEA RISE HOUSE,

GRANDSON OF

SAMUEL THORNTON, M.P.,

AND

MRS. PERCY M. THORNTON,

GRANDDAUGHTER OF

HENRY THORNTON, M.P.

PREFACE

THIS little book appears on the eve of the Centenary of the Abolition of the Slave Trade. The scenes at Clapham in which that 'unwearied, unostentatious, and inglorious crusade' was carried on for twenty years may still be visited; and as we enter Battersea Rise House, which was the head quarters of the campaign, or step inside the parish church, where the Clapham Sect loved to worship, we seem to share the inspiration of those heroic workers. The links between the leaders of the Evangelical Revival and these famous sons of the Church of England were very close. All were moved by the same spirit, and laboured for the same ends.

In these pages indications of sites and houses have been made as clear as possible, so that visitors may be able to find them without difficulty. The last chapter may serve as a guide to those who are strangers to the neighbourhood. It is a great pleasure to be allowed to dedicate this little book to Percy M. Thornton, Esq., M.P., and Mrs. Thornton, who live in the house where Henry Thornton and William Wilberforce carried on their great campaign against the slave trade.

I have gratefully to acknowledge my special debt to Mr. B. R. Tucker for most of the photographs of this volume. Mr. Thornton has allowed photographs to be taken of John Thornton, of Hoppner's painting of Henry Thornton, and of Battersea Rise House. John Thornton's house has been photographed by the kind permission of its present occupants. I owe the illustration of Mr. Wolff's house to the kindness of Mrs. Spokes.

Mr. Grover's *Old Clapham* and Dr. John Venn's *Annals of a Clerical Family* have been carefully consulted. Dr. Venn has kindly read the proof-sheets and given me the benefit of his knowledge of the subject. He has also supplied the portraits of Henry Venn and John Venn and the view of the old parish church of Clapham.

JOHN TELFORD.

CONTENTS

CHAPTER I

CHAPTER II

CHAPTER III

CHAPTER IV

CHAPTER V

CONTENTS

CHAPTER VI

CHAPTER VII

LIST OF ILLUSTRATIONS

Sir James Stephen is still the chief authority for the history of the Clapham Sect. 'Those evangelical saints of his are saints indeed, but they are very human, and it may fall out that the spice with which he embalmed them will preserve their lineaments when the holy men of a newer dispensation are the merest of skeletons.'

MAITLAND's *Life of Leslie Stephen*, p. 16.

The Clapham Sect very wisely abstained from plunging into work for which they were not well qualified, and devoted themselves to work to which they were thoroughly equal. They were men of business, and they devoted their business capacities to the noblest of all purposes. Wilberforce contributed his wonderfully persuasive eloquence, his social influence, his connexion with men of the world of all sorts; Thornton his knowledge of affairs; Stephen his legal acumen; Zachary Macaulay his organizing powers; John Venn his sanctified common sense. They were more or less men of wealth, and they regarded that wealth as literally a talent to be employed in the Master's use; and what was perhaps of hardly less importance, a talent to make the most of, as only business men could do.

OVERTON AND RELTON, *The English Church*, p 235.

CHAPTER I

HENRY VENN AND HIS FRIENDS AT CLAPHAM

'That I may live to the glory of Thy Name!' a petition in Henry Venn's daily Form of Prayer, made the first deep religious impression on his mind. He asked, 'What is it to live to the glory of God? Do I live as I pray? What course of life ought I to pursue, to glorify God?' He walked in the cloisters of Trinity College, Cambridge, as the bell of St. Mary's was tolling at nine o'clock, and 'amidst the solemn tones and pauses of the bell, and the stillness and darkness of the night, would indulge in impressive and awful reflections, on Death and Judgement, Heaven and Hell.'

CHAPTER I

HENRY VENN AND HIS FRIENDS
AT CLAPHAM

A HUNDRED years ago, on March 24, 1807, the House of Lords passed the historic Bill by which the slave trade carried on by British merchants and sailors was brought to an end. The story of the memorable struggle which was then crowned with success is one of the glories of England, and no monuments in Westminster Abbey are more honoured than those of the great Claphamites who had the chief share in the conflict and the victory. They have been commemorated in not a few classic biographies and histories. This little book attempts to set them in their local framework, and to supply a few links in the history which have sometimes been overlooked. It tells a story of God's providence over which Christian men will never cease to wonder; and introduces us to a school in which all labourers for the highest good of the world may learn how to spend their lives to the best purpose. English religion and philanthropy have no brighter page than the story of ' The Clapham Sect.'

How closely the work which found its centre at Clapham is linked to the Evangelical Revival will appear from many incidents in this record.

When John Wesley started the *Arminian Magazine* in 1778, he inserted a selection from his unrivalled correspondence. It began with the letters written by his father and mother in 1725, when he was thinking of entering Holy Orders. Month by month some original document appeared which made Methodism, with its early struggles and victories, stand boldly out before the eyes of a later generation. In November 1797, six years after Wesley's death, a letter is printed, which had been sent to him by a young clergyman. The

writer died on June 24, four months before
the letter was published.   It ran thus :

LONDON, *March* 21, 1754.

'DEAR SIR,—Very shortly (if nothing un-
foreseen prevent) I am to be placed in a
cure near this city, where all the power of
the Spirit of God is especially needful, to
keep me from falling ; and the most press-
ing exhortations of every believer wanted,
to stir me up to diligence and labour.   And
as I have often experienced your words
to be as thunder to my drowsy soul, I
presume, though a stranger, to become a
petitioner, begging you would send me a personal charge, to take heed to feed the flock
committed unto me.   Which will be more
agreeable, if you will found it upon the
declaration of the great Apostle concerning
his inward frame, while he was engaged in
the work of the gospel at Corinth.   As our
commentators are most wretchedly blind,
in explaining the Scripture, I would fain
see the ground of his weakness, and fear,
and much trembling, set forth in your
strong manner.   This will prove, I hope, of

very substantial service to me, and be esteemed an inestimable favour.

'And if you consider, sir, the various snares a curate is exposed to, either to palliate the doctrines of the gospel, or to make treacherous allowances to the rich and great, or at least to sit down well satisfied with doing the least, more than the best, among the idol shepherds—if you consider these things, you will not, I hope, condemn this letter, as impertinently interrupting you in your noble employment, or think one hour lost in complying with its request. It is the request of one who, though he differs from you, and possibly ever may in some points, yet must ever acknowledge the benefit and light he has received from your works and preaching: and therefore is bound to thank the Lord of the harvest, for sending a labourer among us, so much endued with the spirit and power of Elias, and to pray for your long continuance amongst us, to encourage me and my brethren, by your example, while you edify us by your writings.

'I am, sir, your feeble brother in Christ,

'H. Venn.'

The curacy to which Venn refers was that of Clapham, on which he entered the same year. Wesley's private charge to Venn has not been preserved, but there is no doubt that he sent it, for an answer written the same month to a similar request from a friend of Venn's, Samuel Furley, is to be found in the *Christian Miscellany*, 1849. Wesley little dreamt that his correspondent was to become one of the chief guides of the Clapham Sect. Venn wrote in a glow of feeling. The previous morning he had made his first attempt as an extempore preacher at his father's old church, St. Antholin's, where he was lecturer on Wednesday mornings at seven. He describes that as a morning which he long remembered. Venn was the first London clergyman who revived the practice of extempore preaching. Wesley was then in Bristol, recovering from the serious illness which led him to write his own epitaph at Lewisham, and transcribing his *Notes on the New Testament*. He had been silent for four months, but five days after the letter was written he was allowed to preach a sermon. This letter seems to have escaped the attention of Venn's circle. In *Annals of a Clerical Family* (p. 92) it is said that his friendship with Whitefield was of considerably earlier date than that with Wesley.

Wesley's correspondent was the son of Richard Venn, the first London clergyman who refused to allow Whitefield to take his pulpit. An interesting account is given by Tyerman, in his *Life of Whitefield* (i. 172), of a service in St. Margaret's, Westminster, where Whitefield was said to have seized the pulpit and kept out the appointed preacher. Mr. Venn sent a highly coloured report to the *Weekly Miscellany*. Whitefield had been invited to preach for an absent lecturer, but this clergyman had himself secured a substitute, and the arrangement clashed with that made between Whitefield and the Friendly Society.

Richard Venn came of a distinguished family of clergymen who had served the Church of England in uninterrupted succession since William Venn's ordination in 1595. Richard Venn's mother trained him to have the courage of his convictions. She was once asked when she intended to send him to the University, and replied, 'When I have taught him to say "No" boldly.' He learned his lesson and bore a high character at Sidney College, Cambridge. He became a distinguished High Churchman, and enjoyed the friendship of Dr. Gibson, Bishop of London. He was Rector of St. Antholin's, in the neighbourhood of Queen Victoria Street. The church was pulled down about the time that street was made.

Charles Wesley says in his *Journal* for Thursday, December 21, 1738 : ' At St. Antholin's the clerk asked me my name, and said, " Dr. [Mr.] Venn has forbidden any Methodist to preach. Do you call yourself a Methodist?" "I do not; the world may call me what they please." " Well, sir," said he, " it is a pity the people should go away without preaching. You may preach." I did so, on good works.'

Richard Venn married Maria Ashton in 1716. She was the daughter of John Ashton, a gentleman in the court service of James II. He was involved in a Stuart plot, and was executed at Tyburn in 1691.

Richard Venn was a close friend of the first Lord Palmerston, great-grandfather of Queen Victoria's Prime Minister, and fixed his summer residence at Barnes, that he might be near to Palmerston's house at Sheen. Henry Venn was born at Barnes on March 2, 1725. His father died in 1739, at the age of forty-eight.

Henry Venn was trained at Jesus College, Cambridge, where his high spirits, his amiable temper, and his store of anecdotes, 'which he related in a manner peculiarly interesting,' made him very popular. He used often to say that 'he owed the salvation of his soul to the resolute self-denial which he exercised, in following the dictates of conscience in a point which of itself seemed one only of small importance.'

HENRY VENN, M.A.

He was one of the best cricketers in the University, and played in a match between Surrey and All England the week before his ordination. When his side had won the match he threw down his bat, saying, 'Whoever wants a bat, which has done me good service, may take that, as I have no further occasion for it.' When asked the reason for this decision, he replied, 'Because I am to be ordained on Sunday, and I will never have it said of me, "Well struck, Parson."' To this resolution he steadily adhered, though his health suffered for a time from the quieter life he followed.

Henry Venn was elected Fellow of Queen's, and served the curacy of Barton, near Cambridge, for six months before he left the University. Bishop Gibson ordained him deacon in June 1747. In July 1750 he became curate to Mr. Langley, who held the London living of St. Matthew, Friday Street, together with that of West Horsley, near Guildford. Mr. Venn spent part of the summer in London and the rest of the year at West Horsley, where he raised the

number of communicants from twelve to
sixty. His zeal was obnoxious to some of
the neighbouring clergy, but an old fox-
hunting parson silenced the accusers.
'Hush! I feel a great respect for such men
as Mr. Venn, and wish there were more of
the kind! They are the salt of our order,
and keep it from putrefaction. If the
whole body of the clergy were like ourselves,
the world would see that we were of no use,
and take away our tithes; but a few of
these pious ones redeem our credit, and save
for us our livings.'

William Law was now Venn's favourite
author. One day, however, he met a
statement in Law's pages that the blood of
Christ was of no more avail for our salvation than the excellence of His moral character. Venn's eyes were opened. He laid
aside Law, and applied himself more closely
to the study of his Bible. Up to this time
his preaching had been severe, and he in-
sisted on a standard of holiness to which
it was scarcely possible that the frail children of men could ever reach. He now be-

gan to see that we must not rely on perfect obedience, but on the 'all-sufficient merits and the infinite mercies of a Redeemer.' A peace which he had not known before sprang up in his breast, and his preaching became more evangelical.

His son says : ' It is observable that this change of his sentiments was not to be ascribed to an intercourse with others ; it was the steady progress of his mind, in consequence of a diligent and faithful application to the Holy Scriptures, unbiassed by an attachment to human systems. It was not till some years afterwards that he became acquainted with any of those preachers who are usually known by the name of Evangelical ; though his own views now agreed with theirs, and were strictly, and in a proper sense, evangelical—that is, in conformity with the motives and hopes held out to us in the gospel of Christ.'

Henry Venn became curate at Clapham in 1754. Sir James Stonhouse, who held the rectory till 1792, had been appointed in the previous year. Venn ministered in the old parish church of St. Mary. There had been a church here since the twelfth century. It was used till 1776, when the new parish church was opened. The present church on this site is dedicated to St. Paul, and was built in 1815.

One of the old Clapham incumbents was Nicholas Brady (1659–1726), who held the rectory in 1705–6. He and Tate had published their *New Version of the Psalms of David* in 1696. It was denounced as ' fine and modish, flourished with wit and fancy, gay and fashionable '; but whatever faults it had are forgotten as we sing its immortal versions :

' Through all the changing scenes of life.'

' O render thanks to God above.'

'With glory clad, with strength arrayed.'

' How blest is he who ne'er consents.'

'As pants the hart for cooling streams.'

Brady's fame as an eloquent preacher must have lingered in the parish, but Henry Venn has nothing to say about him.

The Atkins' monument in St. Paul's

church still links us to the days of Venn.
Henry Atkins was physician to James I,
and is said to have bought the manor of
Clapham with the present of £6,000 be-
stowed on him by the king after his return
from Scotland, where he had gone to attend
Prince Charles in an attack of fever. His
grandson, Sir Richard Atkins, was buried
in the old Clapham church in 1689.

Manning and Bray described the Atkins'
monument in their *History of Surrey*, but it
totally disappeared for a time. Mr. Grover,
the local historian and antiquary, found a
tradition that it had been stowed away in a
vault on the north side of St. Paul's church.
In December 1885 he had the ground
opened, and discovered the vault with the
marble monument to Sir Richard, his wife,
son, and two daughters. This was restored
and set up in the church after seventy years'
oblivion in the vault.

Many distinguished residents had left
their memory in the village to which Henry
Venn came as curate. In 1663 Sir Denis
Gauden, Victualler to the Navy, erected an

'excellent, usefull, and capacious house on the Common.' Pepys says he built it for his brother, the Bishop of Exeter, who had been promised the diocese of Winchester and wanted this for his town house. Gauden sold it to Mr. Hewer. John Evelyn visited him here on June 25, 1692, and says that he 'got a very considerable estate in the Navy, in which, from being Mr. Pepys' clerk, he came to be one of the principal officers. Mr. Hewer lives very handsomely, and friendly to everybody.' The house had its principal front facing the Common, and stood on the west side of The Chase, where The Terrace and Victoria Road now are. The estate consisted of 432 acres, laid out in the Dutch style, and reached to the grounds of The Cedars and Wandsworth Road. Pepys spent his last days under Mr. Hewer's roof. Evelyn writes on September 23, 1700 : 'Went to visit Mr. Pepys at Clapham, where he has a very noble and well-furnished house, especially with India and Chinese curiosities.' On May 26, 1703, he reports the death of Mr. Pepys, 'who

lived at Clapham, with his partner, Mr.
Hewer, in a very noble and sweete place,
where he enjoyed the fruit of his labour in
great prosperity. He was universally beloved, generous, learned in many things,
and skilled in music ; a very great cherisher
of learned men, of whom he had the conversation.' The house was pulled down about
the time that Mr. Venn became curate.
A little to the west stood another famous
house—The Cedars—beautifully decorated
and said to have been designed by Wren
or Inigo Jones. It was pulled down in
1864.

As curate at Clapham, Venn conducted
a full service on Sunday morning and
preached on Thursday evening. He also
filled three London lectureships—at St.
Alban's, Wood Street, on Sunday afternoon ; on Sunday evenings and Tuesday
mornings at St. Swithin's, London Stone ;
and on Wednesday mornings at seven at
St. Antholin's. We are scarcely surprised
to find that a severe illness in 1756 in-
capacitated him for more than eight months

for public service. His chastening bore good fruit. His whole religious life was deepened during this time of retirement and trial.

It was no doubt through this illness that he was able to attend Wesley's Conference at Bristol in August 1756. The Wesleys and about fifty of their preachers carefully considered the Rules of the Society, 'and all agreed to abide by them all, and to recommend them with all their might.' The rules of the bands and of Kingswood School were also reviewed. Wesley says : 'We largely considered the necessity of keeping in the Church, and using the clergy with tenderness ; and there was no dissenting voice. God gave us all to be of one mind and judgement. My brother and I closed the Conference by a solemn declaration of our purpose never to separate from the Church ; and all our brethren concurred therein.'

Whitefield writes to James Hervey on December 9, 1756 : 'All is well at Clapham. I have expounded there twice.' Venn

went with Whitefield on his preaching-tour
in the West of England in September, 1757.
He was present at Cheltenham in 1768
when Whitefield preached in the burial-
ground to an immense congregation.   Many
were so deeply moved that they burst out
into the most piercing cries.   Venn and
Madan stood up and begged the people
to restrain themselves, and after the
sermon the clergymen present found ample
employment in trying to comfort the
mourners.

When Mr. Venn moved to Huddersfield
the Methodists loved, esteemed, and supported his ministry, though they felt that
their own preachers supplied some elements
which were lacking in his teaching.

Mr. Venn's views became more Calvinistic
in later years, and he did not approve of
Wesley's teaching about Entire Sanctifica-
tion.   He was never an extreme man, and
when asked whether a young minister was
a Calvinist or an Arminian, replied, ' I
really do not know ; he is a sincere disciple
of the Lord Jesus Christ, and that is of

infinitely more importance than his being a disciple of Calvin or Arminius.'

In May 1757, whilst he was curate at Clapham, Mr. Venn married Eling, one of the daughters of the Rev. Thomas Bishop, D.D., minister of the Tower Church, Ipswich. Her son says she was a woman of 'the most sincere and exalted piety, directed by a sound judgement, and enriched by a sweetness of disposition and animation which rendered her particularly interesting, as a companion and a friend.'

Charles Wesley's letters contain several references to the Venns. On July 1, 1755, he writes: 'I spent two hours with Mrs. Venn and Mr. Venn. The former stands her ground as yet.' This is evidently Henry Venn's mother.

On June 7, 1758, he says that he had lately blamed Mr. Venn for his long sermon, but himself preached for near an hour and a half at the Foundery. On July 29, 1759, he took Mrs. Venn with him to dinner at his sister's, Mrs. Wright. He says: 'She has stood her ground against the

whole religious world, and her husband at
their head ; neither can she yet give up her
love, her special love, for the Methodist
people and ministers. She tenderly salutes
you, whom she despairs of seeing again in
the flesh. I am far from confident of
seeing her myself ; but I trust to find her
again in that day, among the children
whom God hath given us.'

Charles Wesley seldom prefixes the year
to his letters, but Dr. John Venn fully
agrees with me that this reference is to
Henry Venn's mother. What a comment
on the position which her husband took
(pp. 22-3) is here !

After dining at Mrs. Wright's, Charles
Wesley rode with Mrs. Venn to Cheapside.
' There she left me in body, not in heart.'
In Mrs. Venn's will, proved July 9, 1762,
she is described as of Bread Street, London.
On February 27, 1759, Charles Wesley was
with Whitefield, Venn, and others at Lady
Huntingdon's, where ' the Lord met us at
His table.' On May 10, 1766, Mr. Venn
breakfasted with him at Mr. Boult's.

Henry Venn referred in his letter to Wesley to the danger of palliating the gospel or making treacherous allowances to the rich and great. That, as he soon discovered, was not what all the rich and great in his new parish expected from a minister of Christ. The most notable man in his congregation was Sir John Barnard (1685–1764) then member of Parliament for the City of London. He held that post of honour in seven successive Parliaments. In 1737 he was Lord Mayor of London. Sir John was a recognized authority on all financial questions, and had refused the post of Chancellor of the Exchequer in 1746. To show their esteem and regard, the citizens of London erected a statue of him in Gresham's Exchange in 1747. Sir John, with characteristic modesty, could not be persuaded to enter the building afterwards.

One beautiful incident will show the spirit of this eminent man. On January 11, 1761, Mr. Venn writes to Mrs. Knipe, sister of Mr. John Thornton: ' Your account of

Mr. John Barnard is very moving. It is re-markable that he was once very much struck with, and seemed not to agree with me in, an observation I made, one Thursday even-ing, to this effect : that if we were without chastening, whereof all are partakers, then are we bastards, and not sons ; that is, the God of heaven and earth neglects our edu-cation, and is provoked to overlook us, as men are wont to do their base-born children. I had more than one or two conversations with him upon the subject, and I suppose the continued prosperity he had met with, the honour and high esteem he was always held in, led him to conclude that he wanted this mark of a child of God. Since this time, you see, the cross has been his portion, and a long season of increasing infirmities and pain, and all the exercises of patience at-tending a lingering but mortal malady, have been appointed to him. I shall be glad to hear of his dismission ; for, sure I am, my eyes have scarce beheld his fellow. Such constant circumspection and such deep humility, such unfeigned Christian love, expressing itself in a total abstinence from evil speaking, is rarely to be found, even amongst the faithful in Christ Jesus. Happy saint! to be so near the glorious transformation. What a mighty and unspeakable change in a moment will he soon feel—from being burdened with a body full of weakness and disease, to enjoy the liberty of a pure spirit; and, from being distracted in the contemplation of his God by a failing memory and a weakened understanding, to hold high and inexpressible communion with the Father of Spirits, without end or interruption ! '

After the death of Sir John Barnard, in 1764, Mr. Venn drew up some brief *Memoirs*. In 1786 these were ' at length published from an impulse of affectionate reverence for his memory, no longer to be resisted, and as a signal instance that one of the first men of his age, and the glory of London, attained this pre-eminence from the best principles which can govern the human mind.'

Another influential member of the Clap-

ham congregation was John Thornton, then a young man of thirty-four. He was the son of Robert Thornton, a merchant in the Russia trade, who lived in an old red-brick house on the south side of Clapham Common. It is the larger and nearer Balham of the two houses now used as the Notre Dame Convent School. It was converted to this use under the auspices of Cardinal Wiseman. There was a farm attached to the property in Clapham Park, where Thornton Road now is. The Thorntons originally came from Yorkshire. John Thornton was born in Clapham on April 1, 1720. He married Lucy Watson, daughter of a merchant in Hull, where she was born in 1722.

Mr. Venn speaks in 1790 of his friend 'first receiving Christ' thirty-six years before. That was in 1754, the year when Venn became curate at Clapham; and makes us ask whether Thornton was a convert of Venn's.

The links between Hull and Clapham were very close. John Thornton's sister married Mr. Wilberforce, uncle of William Wilberforce, who became the chief glory of the Clapham Sect. Wilberforce, of course, was born in Hull ; and there John Venn, Rector of Clapham, and Henry Thornton, found their accomplished wives.

CHAPTER II

VENN AND THORNTON IN LATER LIFE

'Conscious of no aims but such as might invite the scrutiny of God and man, he pursued them after his own fearless fashion—yielding to every honest impulse, relishing a frolic when it fell in his way, choosing his associates in scorn of mere worldly precepts, and worshipping with any fellow Christian whose heart beat in unison with his own, however inharmonious might be some of the articles of their respective creeds.'

SIR JAMES STEPHEN, on John Thornton in *The Clapham Sect.*

CHAPTER II

VENN AND THORNTON IN LATER LIFE

HENRY VENN did not find his work at Clapham altogether encouraging. He says: 'Grieved at the obstinate rejection of the gospel during five years by almost all the rich (and there were very few poor in the place), I accepted a living unexpectedly offered me by my very affectionate friend, the Earl of Dartmouth.' This was the Vicarage of Huddersfield. His wife was very reluctant to leave her friends in Clapham. The vicarage was only worth £100 a year—less than half what his income had been at Clapham; but he thought that living would be considerably cheaper in the north. When he found, after a few months' experience, that he was mistaken, he was almost resolved to return to Clapham; but his wife felt that it was his duty to remain at Huddersfield, and dissuaded him from returning to the south.

When he went to look at the proposed living he wrote to his wife from Huddersfield, on April 15, 1759: 'Tell Mrs. Knipe that leaving her and her dear brother will be a bitter ingredient in my cup. You must assure her there shall be a Mrs. Knipe's room at the Vicarage-house.' Mrs. Knipe expressed her intention of visiting Huddersfield every year, and the confidential letters which passed between her and Mr. Venn show that she still regarded him as her pastor.

In the year of his removal Mr. Venn published a volume of fourteen sermons, dedicated 'To the gentlemen of Clapham, as an acknowledgement of the very many civilities and marks of friendship received by him during the time of his residence amongst them.'

Mrs. Venn died at Huddersfield on September 11, 1767. At the beginning of October Whitefield spent two or three days at the Vicarage to comfort his friend.

Her husband kept his connexion with his old parish and his devoted friends there. In March 1769, when Mr. Thornton was High Sheriff for Surrey, Venn preached at his request the Assize Sermon at Kingston-on-Thames. The text was Zech. ix. 12 : 'Turn you to the stronghold, ye prisoners of hope.' 'Man a condemned prisoner, and Christ the stronghold to save him.' After he left Mr. Thornton's roof, Venn wrote : 'Oh that God would make me, in my sphere, and my dear friend, and every one of us who dwell together, such trees of righteousness as he is! Indeed, his humility can only be equalled by his bounty, and by his watchfulness and diligent use of the means of grace.'

Another sentence shows how he treasured his Clapham circle. 'Thus, by coming at times to be a week or two with my friends, the cement of friendship is maintained.' Mr. Thornton visited him at Huddersfield, and when Venn moved to Yelling he called there in August 1779 on his way to Hull.

Mr. Venn laboured at Huddersfield for twelve years, during which he attained a foremost place among the Evangelical leaders of the day. His preaching made a deep impression. Huddersfield was the first large town outside of London in which Evangelicalism, apart from Methodism, took root.[1]   Venn's *Complete Duty of Man*, a compendium of a Churchman's principles and duties, was a good piece of work, though it never attained the popularity of the *Whole Duty of Man*, which it was intended to supplement and correct.

Venn's friendship with the Evangelical leaders of his day, and his own gospel preaching, brought him much reproach. In 1766 a clergyman asked him to preach, but went off after the service without a word of thanks. 'Who would have thought,' he said, 'that such a cheerful, open countenance as his could have any connexion with Methodism?' The preacher was not without compensation, for two

[1] *History of the English Church.*   Overton and Relton.

persons were awakened by the sermon and became his intimate friends.

On April 18, 1769, he gives another instance of the bitterness among the clergy. 'Last Sunday morning, I preached a charity sermon in one of the largest churches in London. The curate so hated my name, that he left the church, and there was no one to read the prayers : after making the congregation wait, I was obliged to read them myself.'

Some pleasing glimpses are given in his letters of his relations to Lady Huntingdon and John Fletcher, the saintly Vicar of Madeley.

In 1766 Venn visited Brighton. 'I was fired and encouraged by the example of Lady Huntingdon, and dear Mr. Fletcher, who were there.' In November 1769, when doing duty for a few Sundays at the Countess's chapel in Bath, he writes : 'In Lady Huntingdon I see a star of the first magnitude in the firmament of the Church. Blessed be God for free grace, that salvation is to every

4

one that cometh to Christ! otherwise, when I compare my life and my spirit with hers, I could not believe the same heaven was to contain us.'

When Venn met John Fletcher at St. Neots in December 1776, he was so absorbed in the conversation that Fletcher had to remind him of the meal in front of him. From Bath, in June 1777, Venn wrote: ' Dear Mr. Fletcher, who is sinking under a painful disease, accosted me thus: " I love His rod! How gentle are the stripes I feel! how heavy those I deserve! " ' They were both guests of Mr. James Ireland at Brislington. Venn says: ' I was for six weeks in the house with the extraordinary and very excellent Mr. Fletcher. Oh, that I might be like him! I do assure you, that I strictly observed him for six weeks, and never heard him speak anything but what was becoming a pastor of Christ's Church—not a single unbecoming word of himself, or of his antagonists, or of his friends. All his conversation tended to excite to greater

love and thankfulness for the benefits of
Redemption ; while his whole deportment
breathed humility and love. We had many
conversations. I told him, most freely,
that I was shocked at many things in his
" Checks " ; and pointed them out to
him. We widely differ about the efficacy of
Christ's death, the nature of justification,
and the perfection of the saints ; but I
believe we could live years together, as
we did, in great love. He heard me twice ;
and I was chaplain both morning and
evening in the family, as his lungs would
not suffer him to speak long or loud. He
desired his love, by me, to all his Calvinistic
brethren ; and begged their pardon for
the asperity with which he had written.
I am persuaded, as I told him, that if he
were to live with some of those, whom he
has been taught to conceive of as Anti-
nomians, and hear them preach, he would
be much more reconciled to them.' On
Venn's return to Yelling he told his people
from his pulpit that Fletcher was ' like
an angel on earth.'

In 1783 he was at Madeley. He speaks
of 'Mr. Fletcher, a genius, and a man
of fire—all on the stretch to do good—
to lose not a day, not an hour. He is
married to a lady worthy of him—Miss
Bosanquet—a lady with whom I was
acquainted twenty-nine years ago. She
was then sixteen, and brought up in all
the pride of life, her father being one of
the chief merchants of London. By the
grace of God she renounced the world,
from her heart, and gave herself to the
Lord. Since then she has bred up seventy-
four destitute young girls for service, and
seen them placed out to her satisfaction;
and, instead of dressing, visiting, and
conforming to all the vain and expensive
customs of the world, she has been wholly
employed in doing good. I left this happy
house, as Cecil, Secretary to Queen Eliza-
beth, left Bernard Gilpin's, saying, "There
dwells as much happiness as can be known
on earth." '

When he read Fletcher's *Life*, in 1787,
Venn writes: 'What a shining example!

What a proof that zeal, and constant application, and self-denial, can work wonders! What a proof that communications of the Spirit of Christ, though not for merit of anything in us, yet are always in proportion to the pains we take in setting apart solemn times for humiliation, and for seeking after God, that we may have much counsel, direction, and blessing from Him, in our work, and in our souls!' In a letter to Lady Mary Fitzgerald, March 3, 1787, he says that when he thanked Fletcher for two sermons preached in his church at Huddersfield 'he answered, as no man ever did to me, in a way the most affecting I can conceive: with eyes and hands uplifted, he exclaimed, " Pardon, pardon, pardon, O my God! " It went to my very soul: I shall never forget it!' He adds that Fletcher 'thought the day lost, and could find no rest in his soul, unless he was doing good to the bodies and souls of men.'

From Wesley Henry Venn became somewhat estranged as years passed.

He says in 1775: 'Amidst very much error, one great cause of Mr. Wesley's success, some years ago, was his urging Christians not to rest without joy in God from receiving the atonement. Indeed, he erred in making this knowledge to be justifying faith itself, instead of the fruit thereof; and also as to the mode in which the knowledge is required.'

On April 8, 1789, he tells his daughter Catherine: 'I am not sorry you have heard Mr. Wesley—a very extraordinary man, but not to be believed in his assertions about perfection. It is an error, built upon false interpretation of some Scripture passages, in flat contradiction to others which cannot be mistaken. It is an error the Church of Christ has always condemned. It is an error that matter of fact confronts. So far from being perfect, alas! Christians fret and quarrel and fall out, and have so many faults, that if God, as Job speaks of himself, should contend with us, we could not, no, not the best upon earth! answer Him, one of a thousand. "Behold! I

am vile!" belongs to all in the Church.
I hope you were not shaken in your
mind. Never give absolute credit to
what you hear from the pulpit which
is not proved by plain Scripture. How
much more good would Mr. Wesley have
done, had he not drunk in this error!
as there are, doubtless, many very excellent Christians amongst his people; but
the best are sadly harassed by this false
doctrine.'

This shows how far Venn had moved
from Wesley, and how little he really
understood the doctrine which Wesley
taught. Wesley, who says, ' We both like
to speak blunt and plain, without going a
great way round about,' wrote him a
beautiful letter explaining certain points
(*Works*, xiii. 238), but the breach grew.
Canon Overton says: ' " Christian Perfection " is Wesley's designation, "Sinless Perfection " that of his opponents. Guarded,
as Wesley guarded it, it is perhaps a whole-
some and inspiring doctrine, and one which
leads, not to self-righteousness, but to

exactly the opposite result, as is finely expressed in the last stanza of Charles Wesley's noble hymn, attached to his brother's equally noble sermon on Christian Perfection :

> Now let me gain perfection's height !
> Now let me into nothing fall!
> Be less than nothing in my sight,
> And feel that Christ is all in all ! ' [1]

Mr. Venn became Rector of Yelling, about twelve miles from Cambridge, in 1771. He exerted a great influence among his parishioners. One farmer, who had been an infidel, said publicly when he left the neighbourhood : ' Though I have lost more than £200 by my farm here, I shall never repent my coming. I have gained at the church what is worth more than the world.' Venn had been vexed and wretched at his coming, and at the removal of the man whose place he took, but he saw that a providence was in it. Venn's influence was far wider than his parish.

[1] *History of the English Church*, 1714–1800, p. 174.

Many young men from the university, especially young ministers, were accustomed to visit him at Yelling. His son says : ' His powers of conversation were so admirable, his knowledge of religion so extensive, his acquaintance with the world so instructive, and his vigour of mind so great, that, wherever he was, and in whatever company he was placed, every one silently hung upon his lips, and enjoyed the richest feast from his conversation. I lately met with a clergyman, who came over, with two others, to pay him a visit, without any previous acquaintance with him, or any introduction but that which arose from community of sentiment. He told me, that, to the latest hour of his life, he should never forget that conversation ; that it made so deep an impression on him that he did not forget one single sentence ; that, after hearing him converse almost during the whole day, he returned with his companions to Cambridge at night ; and each determined, with an earnestness they had never felt before, to devote themselves unreservedly to the promotion of the gospel of Christ. The party wrote down the heads of that interesting conversation; but, added my friend, "I had no occasion to write it down, for it was impressed indelibly upon my memory; and that day stands distinguished amongst all the other days of my life, like a day spent in Paradise."'

The Rev. Charles Simeon, from his entrance into Orders, had most intimate access to him, and enjoyed much of his company and conversation. 'John Venn,' he says, 'introduced me to his own dear and honoured father, Henry Venn, and oh, what an acquisition was this! In this aged minister I found a friend, an instructor, and a most bright example; and I shall have reason to adore my God to all eternity for the benefit of his acquaintance. How great a blessing his conversation and example have been to me will never be known till the Day of Judgement. I dislike the language of panegyric; and therefore forbear to expatiate upon a character which is, in my estimation, above all praise. Scarcely ever did I visit him, but he prayed with me, at noonday as well as at the common seasons of family worship ; scarcely ever did I dine with him, but his ardour in returning thanks, sometimes in an appropriate hymn, and sometimes in a thanksgiving prayer, has inflamed the souls of all present, so as to give us a foretaste of heaven itself. And in all the twenty-four years that I knew him, I never remember him to have spoken unkindly of any one, but once ; and I was particularly struck with the humiliation which he expressed for it, in his prayer, the next day.' On October 9, 1782, Mr. Venn says that Simeon had been over to see him six times at Yelling within the last three months. 'He is calculated for great usefulness, and is full of faith and love. My soul is always the better for his visits. Oh, to flame, as he does, with zeal, and yet be beautified with meekness!' The Venns introduced Simeon to John Thornton, and probably also to John Newton.

Mr. Venn generally came from Yelling to spend a few weeks in London each year. He preached on Sundays and often in the week. The sermons were largely attended and much blessed.

Meanwhile John Thornton had been pursuing his own path of service. He was 'one of those rare men in whom the desire to relieve distress assumes the form of a master passion.' He inherited a fortune of £100,000 from his father, and became known as one of the rich merchants of Europe. Half his income was devoted to charity. He is said to have induced Dr. Green, Bishop of Lincoln, to ordain John Newton when others had refused to do so, and allowed him £200 a year that he might keep open house when he lived at Olney.

Cowper refers to him as 'John Thornton the Great, who, together with his three sons in Parliament, has, I suppose, a greater sweep in the city than any man.' He wrote some verses in his memory in November 1790. He addresses him as

JOHN THORNTON.

Famed for thy probity from shore to shore—
      Heaven gave thee means
To illumine with delight the saddest scenes,
Till thy appearance chased the gloom, forlorn
As midnight, and despairing of a morn.
Thou hadst an industry in doing good,
Restless as his who toils and sweats for food;
Av'rice in thee was the desire for wealth
By rust imperishable or by stealth.

According to Sir James Stephen, Thornton relished a frolic when it came in his way, and indulged his passion for relieving distress 'with a disdain, alternately ludicrous and sublime, of the good advice which the eccentric have to undergo from the judicious.'

He maintained the most cordial relations with his Nonconformist neighbours. Sir G. O. Trevelyan says : ' Old John Thornton, the earliest of the evangelical magnates, when he went on his annual tour to the south coast, or the Scotch mountains, would take with him some Independent or Wesleyan minister who was in need of a holiday ; and his followers in the next generation had the most powerful motives for maintaining the alliance which he had inaugurated. They could not neglect the doughty auxiliaries in the memorable war which they waged against cruelty, ignorance, and irreligion, and in their less momentous skirmishes with the votaries of the stage, the racecourse, and the card-table.'

The *Memorials* of William Bull, the Independent minister at Newport Pagnell, to whose care John Newton entrusted Cowper when he became Rector of St. Mary Woolnoth, supply a pleasant illustration of this friendly feeling between Churchmen and Nonconformists. Mrs. Wilberforce was with her brother, Mr. Thornton, at Hastings, in September 1782. She wrote to Mr. Bull: 'I long to have you added to my family, as do the rest of us. I have found out a snug place for you to smoke a pipe in, and talk and think on Him who stilleth the waves.' They had three houses for their party, and held religious services in the middle one.

Another illustration is found in the *Life of Joseph Benson*, the Methodist commentator and editor. On June 29, 1817, he preached, from Rev. xiv. 13, on the death of that 'most pious, holy, and useful man, George Cussons,' a leader at Great Queen Street, and read to the congregation a long account of his life and death. As Cussons and his friend John Davies walked home on Friday evening, September 10, 1779, from West Street Chapel, Davies expressed his feeling that something ought to be done for our common soldiers. To his mind nothing seemed so likely to help as giving some of them pocket Bibles which they might read to their comrades. Davies agreed to put his views in a letter which Mr. Cussons promised to send to Mr. Thornton, one of whose almoners he was. He received the following reply :

CLAPHAM, *September* 17, 1779.

'FRIEND GEORGE,—Friend Davies I know not ; but I suppose you do, and his abode, which he does not mention ; and I should join with him in contributing, if he can get a subscription. May the Lord strengthen you in your work, and for your work; and believe me,

'Yours affectionately,

'JOHN THORNTON.'

A little society was formed, to which Mr. Thornton became a liberal subscriber. Out of this grew the Naval and Military Bible Society, which did memorable service in our army and navy, before the British and Foreign Bible Society was formed.

Mrs. Thornton died in 1785. Her husband was spared a few years longer. Henry Venn says in a beautiful memorial discourse, 'The Love of Christ the Source of Genuine Philanthropy,' based on 2 Cor. v. 14, 15, that 'doing good was the great business of his life, and may more properly be said to have been his occupation, than even his mercantile engagements, which were uniformly considered as subservient to that nobler design.' He bears witness that his old friend was 'exact and punctual in the private exercises of the closet.'

In the middle of May 1790 Venn writes :

' On Wednesday I hurried down to Clapham to see Mr. Thornton, who has been suffering greatly from an accident which caused a great loss of blood. However, he is now in good spirits, and has had two good nights. Still, he may feel serious consequences, and his life, seemingly so important to us, be brought to an end.' He died in November at Bath.

Mr. Venn writes: ' I have very sensibly felt the loss of my old affectionate friend, John Thornton, after an intimacy of thirty-six years, from his first receiving Christ, till he took his departure with a convoy of angels, to see Him who so long had been all his salvation and all his desire. Few of the followers of the Lamb, it may be very truly said, have ever done more to feed the hungry, clothe the naked, and help all that suffer adversity, and to spread the savour of the knowledge of Christ crucified!' His son Samuel wrote to Mr. Venn: ' I earnestly pray that his children may follow him in his faith and practice; and may their latter end be like *his* ! which was indeed glorious, through the power of Him who hath conquered death and the grave. My dear father has left you a legacy of £50. He had named you a trustee for his church patronage, in a former will ; but the change was made for your son, as a younger life.' In reporting this to his son, Henry Venn says : 'A ring also was enclosed in the letter. I shall eye it often with a mournful pleasure. No such memorial was needful to remind me of my oldest friend on earth, but one. My parlour, my study, yourself, and his liberal donations to me for many years, are memorials never to be effaced.'

Henry Venn came up to London. 'It was pleasing to hear only of one subject, in all the serious circles—the beloved Gaius, and all his goodness : and the grace, from whence it all flowed, was in every one's mouth.' He rejoiced that he had 'come to see the children of my dear departed friend, John Thornton, and to hear of his life, acts of love, and death.' The nurse told him : 'To see the sons, the day

before he died, weeping tears of grief and
love, and to hear the dying saint affectionately exhort and press each to hold fast
the faith, and to lead the life of a Christian,
was to the last degree affecting. They
asked him whether he was now happy :
" Yes," said he, " happy in Jesus : all
things are as well as they can be ! " And
the last words he was able to articulate
were, " Precious, precious . . . ! " *Jesus*
would have been added, but his breath
failed.'

His daughter, Lady Balgonie, afterwards Countess of Leven, did not see
him for three days before he died, as
she and her children and servants were
suffering from scarlet fever. He was buried
at the north side of the old churchyard.
The Rev. Henry Foster of Camberwell
preached his funeral sermon from the
words, ' Blessed are the dead which die in
the Lord.' John Newton spoke of him in
his own church, and said Mr. Thornton had
given away in acts of love and mercy
£100,000. Mr. Venn thought £150,000,

or an estate of £6,000 a year, would be nearer the truth. 'He has died worth no more than £150,000.' 'At Mr. Henry Thornton's request, I spend, God willing, the next Lord's Day with him, and speak at the old house. "Not," wrote Mr. Wilberforce, " to a mourning family ; but to a family who have abundant cause to rejoice and sing." '

In 1792 Venn says : ' Were there but one thousand loving Christians of great opulence in Britain, like-minded with John Thornton, lately gone to heaven, the nation would be judged and convinced of the good operation of the gospel. Indeed, I sometimes indulge the joyful hope, that the Philadelphian state is approaching, when Christians shall be as much distin-guished by their bowels of compassion, and active love, as by their creed.'

Henry Venn spent his last days in Clapham. John Venn wrote in his diary for 1797 (January 4) : ' My dear father began to occupy his hired house adjoining mine.' That was in Rectory Grove. His eldest daughter, Eling, had married Charles Elliott, of Bond Street, and afterwards of Grove House, Clapham. He was one of the members of the first Committee of the Church Missionary Society, and was an upholsterer. Grove House was near the Old Rectory, and seems to have been pulled down when the Rectory was demolished. John Venn had married Miss King, of Hull, in 1789, and in 1790 his youngest sister Catherine married the Rev. James Harvey. Henry Venn's second wife was dead, and his daughter Jane kept his house. During the last six months he was often on the verge of the grave. His doctor said that the prospect of heaven so elated his mind that it proved a stimulus to life. 'Upon one occasion, Mr. Venn himself remarked some fatal appearances; exclaiming," Surely these are good symptoms!" Dr. Pearson replied: " Sir, in this state of joyous excitement you cannot die." He entered into rest on June 24, 1797.

The poet Cowper said: 'I have seen few men whom I could have loved more had opportunity been given me to know him better; so at least I have thought, as often as I have seen him.' Henry Venn was of middle height and became decidedly stout in later life. He had an open, rather rubicund countenance and extraordinary personal charm.

CHAPTER III

THE CONVERSION OF WILLIAM WILBERFORCE

1774 there were about 240 houses and 1,625 inhabitants; these had grown in 1778 to 344 houses and 2,477 inhabitants. The population rose steadily. In 1801 it was 3,684; 1811, 5,083; 1828, 7,151; and in 1826, 8,588, occupying 1,428 houses. A regular service of coaches was running four times a day to London before the end of the eighteenth century. The coaches carried four inside and ten outside passengers, at fares of eighteenpence inside and a shilling outside. The first coach left for the City at nine. The growth of the village may be seen from the fact that in 1827 the coaches began to run every ten minutes.

The religious life of the place now required a new centre. The old church had become quite inadequate to the needs of the parish, and in 1775 the present church on the common, dedicated to the Holy Trinity, was built at a cost of £11,000. The architect was Mr. Couse. It was ninety feet by sixty, large enough to hold almost the whole population of the parish. It was

CLAPHAM PARISH CHURCH.

opened on June 10, 1776. The present chancel was added in 1902. This church was part of the preparation which the fathers of the Clapham Sect made for their successors.

But they did far more important service in the preparation of the workers who were to win such abiding victories in the cause of religion and philanthropy all over the world. The first place must be given to John Venn, Rector of Clapham, 'to whom the whole sect looked up as their pastor and spiritual guide.' He was himself a native of the village, where he was born on March 9, 1759. William Wilberforce, the great layman of the sect, was born the same year in Hull, on August 24. The clergyman's son grew up in an atmosphere of simple, practical piety, and he did honour to his training.

In July 1773 Henry Venn says that he had determined to put his son under the care of Joseph Milner, the ecclesiastical historian, at Hull for a year. 'He seems, indeed, to be all I could wish, and still continues fixed in his choice of being a preacher of Christ.' In August 1776 he writes : ' I have no fear of my son's abilities ; they are excellent : and I hope he is indeed drawn by grace to desire the ministry. Nothing can be better than his behaviour here. I pray for him day and night ; desiring only one thing, that he may be made an able minister of the New Testament.'

It was just before his ordination in 1782 that young Venn met Charles Simeon, who became his life-long friend.

John Venn was appointed Rector of Little Dunham, in Norfolk, in 1783. On April 29, when he was settled there, his father wrote him a letter which breathes the spirit of the Evangelical Revival : ' You are now to consider yourself as a missionary, sent to teach and preach Jesus Christ. Savages are not more ignorant of His glory and love than are nominal Christians. Look upon your people as prisoners under condemnation ; for whose pardon and recovery you ought to feel, as a tender mother does for the child at her breast. I would have you preach upon the Commandments. God always blesses that preaching.'

John Venn married, in September 1789 Katharine King, daughter of a Hull merchant, and sister to Canon King, of Ely. It is interesting to find that the lady's mother wrote to ask John Thornton's opinion of the suitor. Miss King had been a member of Joseph's Milner's congregation. He told John Venn : ' Many ministers of the gospel are sadly hindered by their wives, who are afraid their husbands would do too much, and cry, " Oh, spare yourself ! " You, sir, have not this to fear : Miss King will be glad to see you wholly given up to your work, and full of zeal for God and for the salvation of sinners.' Mrs. Venn died on April 15, 1803, leaving seven young children.

In 1790 Lady Smythe, whose husband had presented Henry Venn to Yelling, left legacies to him and each of his children. She also gave the advowson of Bidborough, Kent, to John Venn.

The living of Clapham had been held by

Sir James Stonhouse since the year before Henry Venn became his curate there up to 1792. He was the third son of Sir John Stonhouse of Radley, Berks, but his elder brothers, who held the baronetcy in succession, both died without leaving an heir. The rector's successor in the title was his cousin, Dr. James Stonhouse, who had founded the county infirmary at Northampton, and under the influence of Philip Doddridge took Holy Orders in 1749. He was a friend of Hannah More, who wrote of him as the ' Shepherd of Salisbury Plain.' He died in 1795.

When the living at Clapham became vacant on April 13, 1792, through the death of Sir James Stonhouse, the rector, it was offered, according to instructions left by Mr. John Thornton, to the Rev. Henry Foster of Camberwell, ' the friend and assistant curate of William Romaine,' who declined it. The living was then given to John Venn, who was instituted in May 1792. Henry Venn wrote : ' What an honour and lustre is thrown upon

Mr. Foster's character! To what a difficult and dangerous post is my son called! He is in great weakness, fear, and trembling. Now is the time of temptation. Now, more than ever, prayer should be made, that he may glorify God.' John Venn came to live at Clapham in March 1793. He was about five feet seven inches high, slender in youth, but somewhat stout in later life.

The father took a lively interest in his old parish and in all his son's responsibilities.

In September 1794 he says: 'You will oblige me much by writing me the Clapham news. How much do I enjoy your present full employment, and the account of your church being so well attended! I am glad Mr. Grant [of the East India Company] will have no other house but that on Clapham Common. May you be more and more united, and the sons of my old friend, and Mr. Wilberforce; and quicken and excite each other to do much in the service of Christ, and evidently magnify His name!'

On January 1, 1796, Henry Venn says : 'I am not displeased with the opposition of the Huntingtonians to your preaching : their hatred is much to be preferred to their praise. You write, you are well satisfied ; and you have cause to be so ; not only from the full approbation of your friends at Clapham, but from the whole tenor of the Word of God ; for you teach and preach as the Oracles of God. . . . It therefore gives me pleasure to see you stand in the place your father did—pelted on one side by ranters clamouring for sinless perfection, and on the other by Antinomian abusers of grace.'

John Venn established a Sunday evening service at Clapham Church, and was one of the first clergymen to introduce district visiting and parish schools.

It was not only the followers of William Huntington who looked with suspicion on such men as John Venn. The Evangelical party, it has been pointed out, was the strongest spiritual force in the Church of England at the end of the eighteenth cen-

JOHN VENN, M.A.

tury, because there was no other. 'It represented a small minority, either hated or despised by most Churchmen. Bishops regarded Church-Methodism as a disease to be extirpated.' One incident brings this out in a striking fashion. A near relative of Dr. Randolph, the Bishop of London, after being his guest at Fulham Palace, went to visit Mr. Venn at Clapham. The rector sent his son, who afterwards recorded the incident in the *Christian Observer*, to wait at the Bull's Head for the visitor. It was three hundred yards from the rectory in Larkhall Lane [pulled down in 1884], but the prejudice against the Evangelicals was so great that the bishop could not allow his carriage to stop at Mr. Venn's door, though it might be sent to put a lady down at a public-house.[1]

All that the Evangelicals did was viewed with suspicion. Hugh Pearson, afterwards Dean of Salisbury, was almost rejected by the bishop because he spoke favourably of Wilberforce's *Practical View of Christianity*.

[1] *History of Church Missionary Society*, i. 39.

Trinity College, Cambridge, declined to admit Henry Venn's son as an undergraduate. Isaac Milner, then Dean of Carlisle, wrote in August 1813 that Dr. Randolph, the late Bishop of London, was 'most abominably tyrannical and prejudiced up to the ears. His enmity to the Bible Society has been excessive and unreasonable in the highest degree.' He adds that the Bishop of Carlisle had been prejudiced beyond example by Lord Lonsdale, and 'had got it into his head that we are all Dissenters, or little better, at bottom.'

William Wilberforce was born at Hull on August 24, 1759, in an Elizabethan mansion in High Street, then the principal residential quarter. The house was opened as a Wilberforce Museum on August 24, 1906. The boy was sent to the Grammar School kept by Joseph Milner, assisted by his brother Isaac, afterward Senior Wrangler Incomparabilis, and Professor of Mathematics at Cambridge. Even as a schoolboy Wilberforce gave promise of unusual oratorical gifts. 'So rich were the tones of his

voice, and such the grace and impressive-
ness with which it was modulated, that
the Milners would lift him on the table,
that his schoolfellows might admire and
imitate such a model in the art of recita-
tion.'

His father died in 1768, and his uncle,
Mr. Wilberforce of Wimbledon, became his
guardian. He had married a sister of John
Thornton's, who was a friend and disciple
of Whitefield. Their nephew lived with
them at Wimbledon for some time and went
to school there. Mrs. Wilberforce made
him familiar with the Bible and trained him
in habits of devotion. His mother was so
much afraid of these influences that she
called him back to Hull. The boy, who
loved his uncle and aunt as parents, was
almost heart-broken. He was then twelve
or thirteen, and is described by himself as
'completely a Methodist.' He says, 'If I
had staid with my uncle I should have been
a bigoted, despised Methodist.' In this
also he traces the hand of Providence.
The removal, he allows, was the means of

his being connected with political men and becoming useful in life.

On his return to Hull Wilberforce was plunged into a round of pleasures designed to drive out his Methodist notions and make him a man of the world. His mother was a woman of 'real excellence as well as of great and highly cultivated talents, but not possessed at this time of those views of the spiritual nature which she adopted in later life.' She is described as 'an Archbishop Tillotson Christian.'

The honour in which Wilberforce was held in his native town was shown by his election as its member of Parliament in 1780.

Four years later he became representative for the largest constituency in England, the undivided county of York. He soon gained an enviable reputation as a graceful orator. Boswell calls him 'the nightingale of the House of Commons.'

William Pitt became his attached friend, and often came to stay with him at Wimbledon. The young member was a general favourite in society, and seemed well launched on the way to prosperity and favour. But God had chosen William Wilberforce for Himself. The Methodist leaven implanted in his mind and heart by his aunt at Wimbledon was working secretly.

On October 20, 1784, Wilberforce started with his mother, his sister, and two lady relatives on a continental tour. Isaac Milner was with them. Just before this journey Wilberforce casually took up a little volume by Doddridge—*The Rise and Progress of Religion in the Human Soul,* which Mrs. Unwin, Cowper's correspondent, had given to the mother of one of the party. Wilberforce glanced at it hastily, and asked Milner its character. ' It is one of the best books ever written,' he replied, ' let us take it with us and read it on our journey.' Wilberforce gladly consented, and the friends studied it carefully together whilst they were abroad. It led Wilberforce to resolve that at some future time he would examine the Scriptures for himself and see if things were stated there in the same manner. He and Milner returned to England in February 1785. The following July they were together at Genoa, where they began to read the Greek Testament and closely examine its teaching.

A gradual change was taking place in Wilberforce. On November 10, 1785, he got back to Wimbledon. Parliament did not meet till February. Wilberforce spent much of the interval alone holding close communion with his own mind and heart. He says: ' It was not so much the fear of punishment by which I was affected, as a sense of my great sinfulness in having so long neglected the unspeakable mercies of my God and Saviour ; and such was the effect which this thought produced, that for months I was in a state of deepest depression, from strongest convictions of my guilt. Indeed, nothing which I have read in the accounts of others exceeded what I felt.'

He wrote to tell Pitt about his new convictions, and the Prime Minister came out to Wimbledon to talk matters over with him. Then Wilberforce turned to the

venerable John Newton, Rector of St. Mary Woolnoth, for advice in his perplexities.

On December 9 he dined with his aunt, Mrs. Wilberforce. He writes : ' Mr. Thornton there. How unaffectedly happy he is ! Oh that I were like him ! ' On the 21st of the same month he went to Newton's church. The journal notes, ' He has my leave to mention my case to my aunt and Mr. Thornton.'

John Thornton had long been his friend. When Wilberforce was a schoolboy he gave him an unusually large gift of money with an exhortation to bestow some of it upon the poor. Mr. Thornton was not long in acting on the information received. His letter, which has been preserved, is a beautiful revelation of the heart and mind of the old Clapham saint.

To William Wilberforce, Esq.

CLAPHAM, *December* 24 [1785].

'MY DEAR SIR,—You may easier conceive than I can express the satisfaction

I had from a few minutes' converse with
Mr. Newton yesterday afternoon. As
in nature, so in grace, what comes very
quickly forward, rarely abides long. I
am aware of your difficulties, which
call for great prudence and caution.
Those that believe, must not make
haste, but be content to go God's pace,
and watch the leadings of His Providence, as of the pillar and the cloud
formerly. There is a danger in running
from church to church to hear : more profit
is obtained under one or two ministers.
You cannot be too wary in forming con-
nexions. The fewer new friends, perhaps,
the better. I shall at any time be glad
to see you here, and can quarter you,
and let you be as retired as possible,
and hope we shall never be on a footing
of ceremony.

   ' I am, my dear sir,
      ' Your most devoted kinsman,
         ' JOHN THORNTON.'

Wilberforce's journal shows the effect

of this letter. 'By Newton's advice, January 3 [1786], went to Mr. Thornton's; dined with them. J. Thornton perfectly happy and composed. I will go there as often as I dare anywhere.'

A few days later, on the 12th, John Newton came to see his young friend at Wimbledon.

The journal runs: 'Newton staid. Thornton Astell surprised us together on the Common in the evening. Expect to hear myself now universally given out to be a Methodist: may God grant it may be said with truth.'

When he gave up his house at Wimbledon, Wilberforce felt the need of Christian society. He writes: 'Living in town disagrees with me; I must endeavour to find Christian converse in the country.' Mr. Thornton came to his help with the offer of a room in his house at Clapham, where he might live as retired as possible. The offer was heartily accepted, and thus 'the Claphamic system,' that was to lighten so many lives, found its 'sun.'

Henry Venn had his share in the transformation wrought in William Wilberforce. In May and June 1785 he preached each Sunday at Surrey Chapel. He writes: ' I have crowded audiences. Many of the clergy are generally present. The Sub-Dean of the Chapel Royal was there last Sunday, and came into the vestry to speak to me. Mr. Cecil says I do very wrong to come for so short a time. He would persuade me to undertake for half the year. Vain would be the attempt, unless I kept a curate. Mr. Wilberforce has been at the chapel, and attends the preaching constantly. Much he has to give up! And what will be the issue, who can say ? '

Wilberforce's uncle had died in 1771, but his aunt was spared till 1788. She lived at Blackheath, and in the spring of 1786 wrote with deep feeling to the Rev. William Bull about the change that had taken place in the religious views of her nephew. It was a glorious renewal of mind and heart. Sir James Stephen writes that after his conversion, ' God was in all his thoughts. Inhabiting at once the visible and the invisible worlds, he rejoiced over his bright heritage in each.'

CHAPTER IV

THE ABOLITION OF THE SLAVE TRADE

Immediately quit the horrid trade ; at all events, be an honest man. . . . Give liberty to whom liberty is due, that is, to every child of man, to every partaker of human nature. Let none serve you but by his own act and deed, by his own voluntary choice. Away with all whips, all chains, all compulsion !

JOHN WESLEY, *Thoughts upon Slavery*, 1774.

The 'unwearied, unostentatious, and inglorious crusade against slavery' is amongst 'the three or four perfectly virtuous acts recorded in the history of nations.'

LECKY, *European Morals*, i. 160.

CHAPTER IV

THE ABOLITION OF THE SLAVE TRADE

THE toilsome path of duty was now opening before Wilberforce.

He says in 1786 : ' God has set before me two great objects, the suppression of the slave trade and the reformation of manners.' Granville Sharp and Thomas Clarkson had aroused public feeling ; now Wilberforce became the mouthpiece of a growing party. Pitt had been urging him to devote himself to the war against the slave trade. Wilberforce writes : ' Pitt recommended me to take its conduct, as a subject suited to my character and talents. At length, I well remember, after a conversation in the open air at the root of an old tree at Holwood (in 1786), just above the steep descent into the vale of Keston,[1] I resolved to give notice on a fit

[1] A stone seat with these words upon it was placed at this spot by Lord Stanhope in 1862.

occasion in the House of Commons of my intention to bring the subject forward.'

Thus he girded himself for his task, and, as Sir James Stephen says, 'by paths till then untrodden reached a social and political eminence never before attained by any man unaided by place, by party, or by the sword.'

Granville Sharp founded the Society for the Abolition of the Slave Trade in 1787, and the facts brought out as to the horrors suffered by the negroes on board the slave ships led next year to the appointment of a Committee of the Privy Council to make inquiries. Pitt's resolution that Parliament should deal with the question next session was carried unanimously. The number that might be borne in slave-ships was fixed by Act of Parliament.

The crusade against slavery in which Wilberforce was engaged brought him into close contact with the most earnest and enlightened men in England. Two of his friendships have special interest for students of Methodism.

His account of the way he met Charles Wesley at Hannah More's is very beautiful : 'I went, I think in 1786, to see her, and when I came into the room Charles Wesley arose from the table, around which a numerous party sat at tea, and coming forwards to me, gave me solemnly his blessing. I was scarcely ever more affected. Such was the effect of his manner and appearance that it altogether overset me, and I burst into tears, unable to restrain myself.' In 1792, when he heard that Charles Wesley's widow was in poor circumstances, he and two of his friends generously provided her with an annuity of £60, which was paid for thirty years.

Wilberforce writes on February 24, 1789 : 'I called on John Wesley—a fine old fellow.' Wesley says : 'We had an agreeable and useful conversation. What a blessing is it to Mr. Pitt to have such a friend as this !'

It was on May 12 that Wilberforce opened the debate on the slave trade in a noble speech three hours and a half long.

7

James Rogers, who was with Wesley on his
last little tour to Leatherhead, says that 'the
night following we stopped at Mr. Wolff's,
at Balham, on our return home. At these
places Wesley rested comfortably, and rose
each morning at four o'clock, it being his
usual hour of rising for more than sixty
years. On the Friday morning, after retiring half an hour, he desired me to read
to him part of the account just then
published, on the sufferings of the poor
negroes in the West Indies; and before
breakfast, to write a letter to a friend in
Cork, which was the last he ever dictated;
and it was with the utmost difficulty he
signed his name; nor did this eminent
writer ever after use the pen.'

The previous night he had written another letter, which has become a classic.
Wilberforce heard no 'Well done' on
earth more inspiring than that which
came from John Wesley.

LONDON, *February* 24, 1791.

' MY DEAR SIR,—Unless the Divine Power

has raised you up to be as Athanasius, *contra mundum,* I see not how you can go through your glorious enterprise in opposing that execrable villany which is the scandal of religion, of England, and of human nature. Unless God has raised you up for this very thing, you will be worn out by the opposition of men and devils ; but *if God be for you, who can be against you* ? Are all of them together stronger than God ? Oh, " be not weary in well-doing ! " Go on, in the name of God and in the power of His might, till even American slavery, the vilest that ever saw the sun, shall vanish away before it.

'Reading this morning a tract, wrote by a poor African, I was particularly struck by that circumstance that a man who has a black skin, being wronged or outraged by a white man, can have no redress ; it being a law in our colonies that the *oath* of a black against a white goes for nothing. What villany is this !

'That He who has guided you from your youth up may continue to strengthen you in this and all things is the prayer of, dear sir, your affectionate servant,

'JOHN WESLEY.'

Shortly afterwards, on April 18, Wilberforce brought in his Bill for the Abolition of the Slave Trade, but it was defeated by 163 votes to 88.

Wilberforce's introduction to the Thornton household at Clapham bore lasting fruit. The youngest of John Thornton's sons had met in his father's house those who made great profession of religion but were dishonourable in their daily conduct. He says, ' This so disgusted me that, had it not been for the admirable pattern of consistency and disinterestedness which I saw in Mr. Wilberforce, I should have been in danger of a sort of infidelity.' Henry Thornton and Wilberforce formed a warm friendship. In 1792, two years after John Thornton's death, Wilberforce says: ' Henry Thornton has bought Lubbock's house at Battersea Rise, and I am to share it with him, and pay so much per annum towards expenses. Last night I went over the house with Grant and Henry Thornton. How thankful I should be, to whom it is the only question which of many things, all comfortable, I shall choose!' Mr. Lubbock, an ancestor of Lord Avebury, sold Battersea Rise House to Mr. Akerman, from whom Henry Thornton purchased it. The house was everything that could be desired. It was wreathed with honey-suckle and wistaria, and looked across an extensive lawn, studded with aged elms and massive tulip-trees, to distant vistas of open fields and forest-trees. 'Single-speech Hamilton,' whose maiden speech as member for Petersfield in 1755 eclipsed all his subsequent speeches, once lived in this house. He was for some time Chancellor of the Irish Exchequer.

The principal sitting-room, known as the library, is a lofty oval saloon said to have been designed by Pitt on one of his visits to his brother-in-law, who was Mr. Thornton's tenant at Broomfield. The room was curiously wainscoted with books on every side, except where it opened on the lawn.

Thornton and Wilberforce were both bachelors at this time. Battersea Rise exactly met their idea of a quiet retreat where they might spend the week-end in devotion and helpful intercourse with congenial companions. Henry Thornton was a banker in Bartholomew Lane, and member of Parliament for Southwark. He inherited his father's philanthropic spirit, and before his marriage gave away six-sevenths of his income. The amount in some years exceeded £9,000. Even after his marriage his smallest annual gifts reached £2,000. He was the author of the famous *Family Prayers*. They were prepared for use in his own household. Some who heard them there expressed a desire that they should not be confined to that circle. An imperfect edition was printed, but in 1834 Sir Robert H. Inglis published another edition. There are twenty-eight morning, twenty-three evening prayers, with five each for Saturday evening, Sunday morning and Sunday evening.

Mr. G. W. E. Russell says his own father always read a chapter of the Bible, morning and evening, and after it one of Thornton's Family Prayers; 'indeed, the use of that book was a distinctive sign of true Evangelicalism.'

He tells an amusing story of a worthy baronet who ventured on extemporary prayer, and 'went so far as to invite contributions from the servants. As long as only the butler and the housekeeper voiced the aspirations of their fellows, all was decorous; but one fine day an insubordinate kitchen-maid took up her parable, saying: "And we pray for Sir Thomas and her ladyship, too. Oh, may they have new hearts given to them!" The bare idea that there was room for such renovation caused a prompt return to the lively oracles of Henry Thornton.'

Zachary Macaulay thus compares his two friends: 'Wilberforce has stronger and more lively views of the beauties of holiness and of the Saviour's love ; but Thornton has a more uniform and abiding impression of his accountableness to God for every moment of his time, and for every word he utters.'

Henry Thornton had blue eyes and a strong Saxon face. Sir James Stephen describes him as a man of judicial nature. ' Brows capacious and serene, a scrutinizing eye, and lips slightly separated, as of one who listens and prepares to speak, were the true interpreters of the informing mind within.' Nothing which fell within the range of his observation escaped his judicial examination. ' To investigate the great controversies of his own and of all former times, was the chosen employment : to pronounce sentence on them, the dear delight of his leisure hours.'

He was not a man of any creative faculty, and apart from his glorious band of helpers he would not have accomplished any startling result ; but he may justly be described as the backbone of all the enterprises undertaken by the Clapham Sect.

When Wilberforce became immersed in

THE LIBRARY, BATTERSEA RISE HOUSE.

PERCY M. THORNTON, ESQ , M.P.

his historic philanthropies it was hard for him to secure quiet. In 1794 he says: 'I find that I must as little as is really right ask people to Battersea Rise to stay all night, as it robs and impoverishes the next morning. I had meant this for a fast day, but it has been broken in pieces in this way.' Hannah More visited the two bachelors here in 1794. She writes to her sister about the care which 'the two masters' took of her, the carriages placed at her disposal, and the pleasant company.

The masters of Battersea Rise had much happy intercourse with John Venn. One night, in 1796, he came across the Common, as Wilberforce notes in his journal, 'and told us his grief that a new chapel was talked of, because he did not preach the gospel! We discussed, and told Venn his faults; but he acknowledged, and we too, who much agree with him, that he does not agree with any of the gospel preachers. They swell one part to the lessening of another; strain and pervert Scripture.'

Henry Thornton was a man of deeds,

not of words. Zachary Macaulay tells Miss Mills, October 1797 : ' Mr. Thornton's letter, in which were only eight lines, was long enough to give me the satisfaction of knowing that he had nothing particularly to blame ; a negative, but from Henry Thornton no mean praise.' He adds, that when he was in England Mr. Thornton's ' mind was in a most tumultuary state at the time, and even when talking to him on serious business he would all at once interrupt the conversation by proposing some question, or entering into some details respecting Miss Sykes.'

Thornton's marriage to this lady made Wilberforce homeless for a time, but he soon found a congenial dwelling close to his friend.

When he took possession of the property, Mr. Thornton had enlarged Battersea Rise and built two other houses on the estate. The nearest of these, standing on its west side, was let to Mr. Charles Grant, the Chairman of the Board of Directors of the East India Company. He had been in the service of the Company, and returned home in 1790. Sir James Stephen speaks of his stately figure and the calm dignity of his spacious brows, well befitting the real ruler of the rulers of the East. The name of this residence, Glenelg, keeps alive the memory of his eldest son. In this house the Rev. William Arthur lived for many years, after his return from Belfast. He died at Cannes on March 9, 1901, and a memorial tablet is fixed at the entrance of the Clapham Wesleyan church, of which he was one of the chief supporters.

The other house—Broomfield, as it was called till Sir Charles Forbes, who lived there from 1851 to 1877, changed it to Broomwood—was separated from Battersea Rise by shrubberies. It was first occupied by the Hon. Edward Eliot, who married Pitt's sister, Harriet. When she died, in September 1786, Wilberforce wrote: 'I don't believe there ever existed between brother and sister a more affectionate attachment than between Pitt and Lady Harriet.' The statesman used to spend his holidays here.

In 1797 Wilberforce rented Mr. Eliot's house as an occasional retreat.   Eliot died the same year.   This was a great loss to Wilberforce, 'for except Henry Thornton there is no one living with whom I was so much in the habit of consulting, and whose death so breaks in on all my plans in all directions.'

After his marriage Wilberforce fixed his home at Broomfield.   The house was pulled down in 1904.   A tablet in Wroughton Road marks its site, and its memory is preserved by Broomwood Road.

In the year that he entered on possession of Broomfield, Wilberforce published *A Practical View of the Prevailing Religious System of Professed Christians in the Higher and Middle Classes in this Country, contrasted with Real Christianity*.   That was his attempt to fulfil the great task of the reformation of manners which he felt that God had set before him.   His aim was to show the scanty and erroneous system of most orthodox Christians, and contrast it with what the author regarded as real

HENRY THORNTON, M.P.
From a painting by Hoppner, presented to Mr. Thornton by his constituents
in Southwark.

Christianity. Within six months 7,500 copies of the work were sold, and in England and America edition followed edition. It bore notable fruit.

At Broomfield, in 1799, he writes : ' Heard to-day of a clergyman in the Isle of Wight to whom my book was blessed. Oh, praise, praise ! ' This was Legh Richmond, who wrote the touching record of *The Dairyman's Daughter*, which has been blessed to the conversion of multitudes.

In 1798 Wilberforce goes ' to town directly for Methodists' sake,' to help them to resist the measure for Sunday drill in the Channel Islands. Every one wanted his support. Henry Thornton speaks of ' the heap of fellows ' that troubled him. He thought of giving up his villa that he might have more money for the poor. Already he gave away a fourth of his income. At Broomfield he was 'incessantly worried with company.' But he had compensations : ' The nightingales are abundant.' They have long since taken flight, though they have left their memory in ' Nightingale Lane.'

Wilberforce was the soul of all the social gatherings at Battersea Rise. Bishop Jebb, 'the learned, great, and pious Bishop of Limerick,' said he 'had the face of an angel and the agility of a monkey.'

In *Wilberforce and his Friends* Mr. J. C. Colquhoun describes a May evening in Henry Thornton's garden when mothers and children gathered on the lawn : ' Presently, streaming from adjoining villas or crossing the Common, appeared others who, like Henry Thornton, had spent an occupied day in town, and now resorted to this well-known garden to gather up their families and enjoy a pleasant hour. Hannah More is there, with her sparkling talk ; and the benevolent Patty, the delight of young and old ; and the long-faced, blue-eyed Scotchman (Charles Grant), with his fixed, calm look, unchanged as an aloe-tree, known as the Indian Director, one of the kings of Leadenhall Street ; and the gentle Thane, Lord Teignmouth, whose easy talk flowed on, like a southern brook, with a sort of drowsy murmur ; and Macaulay stands by listening, silent, with hanging eyebrows ; and Babington, in blue coat, dropping weighty words with husky voice ; and young listeners, starting into life, who draw round the thoughtful host, and gather up his words— the young Grants, and young Stephen, and Copley, a " very clever young lawyer."

'But whilst these things are talked of in the shade, and the knot of wise men draw closer together, in darts the member for Yorkshire, from the green fields to the south, like a sunbeam into a shady room, and the faces of the old brighten, and the children clap their hands with joy. He joins the group of the elders, catches up a thread of their talk, dashes off a bright remark, pours a ray of happy illumination, and for a few minutes seems as wise, as thoughtful, and as constant as themselves. But this dream will not last, and these watchful young eyes know it. They remember that he is as restless as they are, as fond of fun and movement. So, on the first youthful challenge, away flies the volatile statesman. A bunch of flowers, a ball, is thrown in sport, and away dash, in joyous rivalry, the children and the philanthropist.   Law and statesmanship forgotten, he is the gayest child of them all.'

Battersea Rise was the head quarters of the Clapham Sect, where all its projects were discussed and matured ; but one of its most active and zealous members lived across the Common on the edge of what is now the High Street.

Zachary Macaulay was born in 1768 at Inverurie, where his father was then minister. There was a large family at the Manse, and Zachary was placed in a merchant's counting-house in Glasgow at the age of fourteen. He had a strong desire for a college training, but his father could not afford the expense. He had already gained by his own exertions a good knowledge of Latin, Greek, and French, and had made considerable progress in mathematics. He was also an insatiable reader, and had such a memory that when Wilberforce was at a loss for a piece of information in later days, he would say, 'Let us look it up in Macaulay.' Before he was seventeen he was sent, at his own request, to push his fortunes in Jamaica. He became book-keeper on a sugar plantation, where the punishment inflicted on the negroes made his blood run cold. He set himself to conquer his squeamishness, and in 1785 alludes to himself as 'cursing and bawling' in a field of canes amidst perhaps a hundred negroes, 'while the noise of the whip resounding on their shoulders, and the cries of the poor wretches, would make you imagine that some unlucky accident had carried you to the doleful shades.' He did his utmost for some years 'to alleviate the hardships of a considerable number of my fellow creatures, and to render the bitter cup of servitude as palatable as possible.'

His grandson, Sir George O. Trevelyan, adds other particulars.

'He had read his Bible too literally to acquiesce easily in a state of matters under which human beings were bred and

8

raised like a stock of cattle, while outraged morality was revenged on the governing race by the shameless licentiousness which is the inevitable accompaniment of slavery. He was well aware that these evils, so far from being superficial or remediable, were essential to the very existence of a social fabric constituted like that within which he lived.'

Zachary Macaulay was saved 'from the vulgar practices and manners which disgraced almost every rank of men in the West Indies'; yet there is little doubt that he was becoming hardened to the suffering around him, when an offer of employment brought him back to England just as he had completed his twenty-first year. His favourite sister had married Thomas Babington, of Rothley Temple, and her husband set himself to help his young relative, and led him to Christ.

He came home in time to render eminent service to the Clapham philanthropists. Henry Thornton had taken an active share in all the arrangements for founding a colony at Sierra Leone for liberated slaves. He formed the company, got together the capital, drew up the constitution and was Chairman of the Board of Management of which Wilberforce, Granville Sharp, Grant, Stephen, and three more Thorntons were members.   Babington told Henry Thornton of Zachary Macaulay and his experience in the West Indies. Macaulay paid a visit of inspection to Sierra Leone in 1791, and in January 1793 went out as second member of the Council for the management of the little colony.   He became Governor in March 1794.

On his return to England, in 1795, Macaulay arranged to sail in a slave-ship, the *Mary*, in order that he might see what the wretches had to bear.   The captain treated the slaves with a certain amount of kindness, but to Macaulay those three weeks were a time of torture.   He wrote to a friend: ' During the night I hung over a crowd of slaves huddled on the floor, whose stench at times was almost beyond endurance.   There was no possibility of my having any exercise—the quarter-deck was so fully occupied by slaves during the day as to render it difficult to move without treading on them. . . . If my state was so uncomfortable, what must theirs have been whom I saw around me, extended naked on the bare boards, fettered with irons; deprived of every means of chasing away the gloom of confinement; unable, when sick, to reveal the cause of their complaints; strangers to any portion of that blessed and heart-cheering hope which makes the slave a free man; ignorant of the fate which awaited them; filled with fears either of a horrid death or a cruel servitude, and without the most distant prospect of visiting their native land, or beholding the face of one of those friends and relatives from whom they had been forcibly torn. And what are we more than these ? Are not these also, even these, abject as they seem, the purchase of a Saviour's blood, and graven upon the palms of His hands ? ' [1]

[1] *Christian Observer*, 1839.

The horrors of the middle passage were so great that out of every hundred negroes put on board the slave-ship in Africa only half lived to become labourers on the other side of the Atlantic.

The *Gentleman's Magazine* for February 1906 gives extracts from the ledger kept by the captain of a Liverpool slaver in 1785–7. In 1771 there were 195 English slave-ships, capable of carrying 47,146 negroes. Liverpool had 107 ships, London 58, Bristol 25. The ship of which John Newton was captain is entered in 1753 as carrying 250 slaves. In 1786 the average number of slaves taken from Africa was 100,000, of whom English ships carried about 42,000. The largest English ship carried 1,200. 'A prime Gold Coast man would sell for £36 sterling in the West Indies.' The slaver's ledger gives the grim details of this traffic. Each slave is numbered, and the height and sex are noted, with a list of the articles given in exchange. One item is 'seven small boys and one girl.' Another entry runs:

'Bartered with Captain Vernier one man-boy for sixty gallons brandy.'

On a visit to Cowslip Green, the home of Hannah More, in 1796, Macaulay met Selina Mills, the daughter of a retired bookseller in Bristol, who was a member of the Society of Friends. Miss Mills had been a pupil at the school kept by Hannah More and her sisters. She was born in 1767, and was 'extremely pretty and attractive,' with a sweet temper and retiring disposition. Macaulay did not intend to declare his affection, but seeing the young lady weeping bitterly in a room as he left Cowslip Green, he gave expression to his feelings and was not left in doubt as to the regard which he had inspired in her breast. Miss Patty More was jealous of such a rival in her friend's affection, but the attachment was proof against such opposition. On the eve of his departure to Sierra Leone, Zachary Macaulay sent Miss Mills a small Methodist hymn-book which, he says, 'was my companion in hunger and nakedness and distress. We must no

doubt make many allowances for the
peculiarities of Methodism ; but on the
whole, as the frequent marks of approbation will show you, it pleases me much.
One of them, beginning, " Give to the
winds thy fears," has often cheered my
mind as I viewed the desolation caused by
the French visit. And another, " God of
my life, whose gracious power," scarce ever
recurs to my mind without causing it to
swell with grateful recollection.' Macaulay
had completely lost his heart, for he tells
her : ' Were the possession of anything the
world deems good brought into competition
with Selina Mills, I would reject it without
the smallest hesitation.'

Part of Macaulay's duty in England was
to complete the arrangements for the
Wesleyan Methodist Mission to the Foulah
nation. ' The Directors had undertaken
that this Mission should have a free passage
in the *Calypso,* one of their vessels, and
should be started in Africa under the
auspices of their Governor.' The duty had
its drawbacks. He tells Miss Mills from

Portsmouth, February 12, 1796: 'I am pestered almost to death with Dr. Coke and his missionaries.'

Macaulay resigned his governorship in 1799, and married Miss Mills on August 26. Their first two years of married life were spent at the offices of the Sierra Leone Company in Birchin Lane, Cornhill.

In 1802 the Macaulays moved to Clapham. Mrs. Macaulay always preferred a book to company, and it was somewhat a disappointment to her husband that she did not mix much in the social gatherings at Clapham, though at first she regularly accompanied him to Battersea Rise and Broomfield on Saturdays.

When he gave up his post in Sierra Leone Zachary Macaulay brought home a company of negro children. On June 1, 1799, he writes from Battersea Rise: 'On Wednesday my black children got to Clapham in good health, and excited no small admiration among our friends, who account them a highly favourable specimen of African youth. Mrs. More, who is still an

inmate of Battersea Rise, began to cate-
chize one of them a little, and was much
pleased with his ready answers, though I
find on an examination which I instituted
this morning that they have rather lost
ground during our separation. They live
about a mile hence in the village of St.
Pancras. I have been to the smallpox
hospital (in St. Pancras) to arrange for
their all being sent thither for inoculation.'
A little later he visited them at the hospital,
where he found that great attention was
paid them. He gives an amusing account
of Mr. John Campbell, a missionary friend,
escorting the youngsters across the Common
to Battersea Rise. On arriving at Mr.
Henry Thornton's gate, he was alarmed to
find some of his charge missing. ' It arose
from companies dining in the neighbouring
mansions, astonished to see a cloud of
young Africans, sending out their men-
servants to try and catch some of them and
bring them before them. They fancied all
were their friends, and most willingly went
with any who asked them.' John Venn

and Henry Thornton brought William Greaves from Yorkshire to teach the negro children, but the climate proved fatal, and by the end of 1805 only six were alive.

A writer in the *Christian Observer*, 1872, describes a visit which he paid one Sunday afternoon at Zachary Macaulay's request to the African Seminary. The negro boys stood in a semicircle round Macaulay, who examined them. Henry Thornton was at his side, while Wilberforce, on the outside of the group, went from boy to boy patting them on the shoulders as they gave good answers to the questions, and adding a few words of encouragement and admonition to teach the same truths to their countrymen. Eight of the boys were subsequently baptized at Clapham Church by John Venn in 1805.

Zachary Macaulay won the esteem and affection of all Christian men. On January 12, 1802, Joseph Benson says: 'I dined with Mr. Pearson of Golden Square, and afterwards spent an agreeable hour with him and Mr. Macaulay, late Governor of Sierra

Leone, who seems a truly pious man. At seven I preached at Grosvenor Chapel.'

Zachary Macaulay was one of the most devoted and unselfish men of his generation. With an 'ineloquent tongue' and 'taciturn features,' he had a heart of gold. Despite 'the most bitter, scurrilous, and persistent attacks from the defenders of slavery,' he toiled on, refusing even his just share of honour and praise.

The inscription on his tablet in Westminster Abbey, which was written by Sir James Stephen, describes him truly as one

> Who during forty successive years,
> Partaking in the counsels and the labours
> Which, guided by favouring Providence,
> Rescued Africa from the woes,
> And the British Empire from the guilt,
> Of Slavery and the Slave Trade,
> Meekly endured the toil, the privation, and the reproach,
> Resigning to others the praise and the reward.

Sir Henry Taylor says that Wilberforce's gifts 'placed his name in the title-page (as it were) of a great cause. But Mr.

Zachary Macaulay was the man who rose and took his pen in hand at four o'clock in the morning.' His grand-daughter, Viscountess Knutsford, who died in August, 1906, has painted a noble portrait in her *Life and Letters of Zachary Macaulay.*

The Liverpool merchants and those who were interested in the slave trade made a stout resistance, in 1792, to Wilberforce's motion for its immediate abolition, and succeeded in carrying a plan for gradual abolition. It was stipulated that the trade should cease entirely in 1795 or 1796. The Opposition managed to delay the measure from year to year, and it was not till March 1807 that Parliament resolved that the slave trade should come to an end on January 1, 1808.

Granville Sharp (1735–1813) was the most picturesque member of the Clapham Sect. He lived in the house in Church Buildings, over the eastern archway. Sir James Stephen says that ' as long as Granville Sharp survived it was too soon to proclaim that the age of chivalry was done.'

The grandson of an archbishop of York and son of a prebendary of Durham, he served his time with a draper on Tower Hill, and for eighteen years (1758–1776) was a clerk in the Ordnance Office. Whilst in this humble position he fought out the series of actions which led in 1775 to the classic decision which lay at the root of the anti-slavery movement, ' that as soon as any slave sets foot upon English territory he becomes free.' This signal victory was due in the first instance to Granville Sharp's sympathy with a negro in 1765, who had been left to starve in his sickness and disease. He asked for alms. Sharp secured medical aid and watched over the sufferer till, by a kind of miracle, he recovered. Then his master, Mr. Lisle, of Barbados, brought an action for the illegal detention of his property. Sharp fought the case. In 1772 a full bench of judges decided that the negro was under the protection of England and was no longer the property of Mr. Lisle. Thus a homely, obscure philanthropist, by his own devotion and by his research into English law, emancipated for ever the negro who was resident on English soil, and 'in fact banished slavery from Great Britain.' That marked him out as 'the father of the movement.' He was Chairman of the Society for the Abolition of Slavery founded in 1787, and as Bishop Porteus said : ' The first publication which drew the attention of the country to the horrors of the African slave trade came from his pen.'

One of the most powerful advocates of emancipation and the abolition of the slave trade was James Stephen, who had practised as a barrister in the West Indies, where he had influential relatives at St. Christopher's. He says that he was led by an acquaintance accidentally formed to sail in a vessel which touched at Barbados in December 1783, where he was present at the trial of four negroes on a charge of murder. The way they were treated opened his eyes to the horrors of slavery. He got to know Wilberforce, when he visited England in 1788, and in 1794 resigned his position at the West Indian Bar, which his views on the slave question had made intolerable.   His experience and legal training made him an invaluable ally in the great crusade.   He even ventured frankly and kindly to reprove Wilberforce in 1798 'for not pleading the cause of the slaves watchfully enough, and guarding it in the case of Trinidad, and Spain's late proposals.' When Wilberforce hesitated to attack certain proposals of the Government, this zealous friend did not hesitate to tell him he had been 'improperly silent.'   In 1800 Mr. Stephen, who was a widower, married Wilberforce's only sister, the widow of Dr. Clarke, Vicar of Holy Trinity, Hull. About 1807 he accepted a seat in Parliament offered him by his old and intimate friend, Mr. Perceval.   He originated the 'Orders in Council,' which, Lady Knutsford says, 'made his name justly famous, and contributed during the next few years to undermine the power of Napoleon in almost an equal degree with the force of our arms.' Mr. Stephen was a man of great natural gifts, of unflinching courage and force of character. He died at Bath in 1832, 'almost in the presence of Wilberforce, who only survived his old friend by a few months.'

The Bill for the Abolition of the Slave Trade was carried on February 23, 1807, by 283 votes to 16, and sent to the House of Lords on March 18. Wilberforce wrote: 'Never surely had I more cause for gratitude than now, when carrying the great object of my life, to which a gracious Providence directed my thoughts twenty-six or twenty-seven years ago, and led my endeavours in 1787 or 1788.' The House of Commons was enthusiastic. When Sir Samuel Romilly entreated the young members to let the day's event be a lesson to them, how much the rewards of virtue exceeded those of ambition, and contrasted the feelings of the Emperor of the French 'in all his greatness with those of that honourable individual, who would this day lay his head upon his pillow and remember that the slave trade was no more,' the whole House, surprised into a forgetfulness of its ordinary habits, burst forth into acclamations of applause. They had watched the labours of Wilberforce for twenty years, and rejoiced that they were now crowned by such a magnificent victory. The Bill was passed by the House of Lords on March 24, and next day received the Royal Assent. It was the last act of the administration of Lord Grenville.

When the slave trade was abolished, Zachary Macaulay, in connexion with Wilberforce, Stephen, and others, founded the African Institution to promote the interest of the negro and watch over the working of the Abolition Bill. Zachary Macaulay was Honorary Secretary, Several Acts of Parliament were secured to improve the condition of the negro, and every European nation was induced to declare the slave trade illegal. Another association, the London Anti-Slavery Society, was also founded by Macaulay to supplement the work of the African Institution, and do more popular and aggressive service.

When Parliament abolished slavery at

9

a cost of twenty millions sterling in 1833, Thomas Fowell Buxton wrote to Zachary Macaulay : 'Surely you have reason to rejoice. My sober and deliberate opinion is that you have done more towards this consummation than any other man. For myself, I take pleasure in acknowledging that you have been my tutor all the way through, and that I could have done nothing without you.'

Mrs. Macaulay died in 1831, and her husband on May 13, 1838. Sir James Stephen wrote to Miss Fanny Macaulay : 'I know not how to grieve for the loss of your father, though it removes from this world one of the oldest, and assuredly one of the most excellent friends I have ever had. What rational man would not leap for joy at the offer of bearing all his burdens, severe as they were, if he could be assured of the same approving conscience, and of the same blessed reward ? He was almost the last survivor of a noble brotherhood now reunited in affection and in employment. Mr. Wilberforce, Henry Thornton,

Babington, my father, and other not less
dear, though less conspicuous, companions
of his many labours, have ere now greeted
him as their associate in the world of
spirits ; and, above all, he has been wel-
comed by his Redeemer with " Well done,
good and faithful servant." '

Methodism had a vital share in that
work for the slaves which lay so near to
the heart of Wilberforce and his helpers.
Dr. Coke first visited Antigua in 1786.
He found there a large Methodist congregation of negroes under the care of John
Baxter, a naval shipwright and local
preacher. From that time the work grew
rapidly. One of the most useful and
popular preachers was a slave called Black
Harry, who was publicly whipped, im-
prisoned, and banished from St. Eustatius
for the crime of praying with his coloured
brethren. Coke came to England for missionaries and collected funds for the work
from door to door. Persecution soon arose
from the planters and white people, who
were living in a state of open immorality.

One of the Methodist missionaries, John Stephenson, was thrown into prison for preaching in Jamaica. Similar outrages were committed on Methodist missionaries in other places. A law was passed in Jamaica forbidding any 'Methodist missionary or other sectary to instruct slaves, or receive them into their houses, chapels, or conventicles of any sort.' This was rescinded on the appeal of Dr. Coke and the Missionary Committee to the Home Government.

All this brought Methodism into close touch with the Clapham Sect. It furnished material for the appeals of Wilberforce and his friends to Parliament and to the country, and enlisted all the forces of a growing church on the side of liberty.

In 1791 Wilberforce appealed formally to the Methodist Conference for assistance in his crusade, and obtained a promise of all that he wanted. He had previously sent a printed letter and a copy of the evidence given before his Select Committee to every Methodist preacher.

Methodism had an even larger share in the struggle which Sir Thomas Fowell Buxton led to victory. When the Abolition Bill of 1807 made the slave trade illegal the Methodist Conference set its face steadily in the direction of Emancipation. It determined in its annual meeting at Liverpool in August 1807 ' that none of our preachers employed in the West Indies shall be at liberty to marry any person who will not previously emancipate, in the legal methods; all the slaves of whom she may be possessed: and if any of our brethren there, already married, have, by such marriage, or in any other way, become proprietors of slaves, we require those brethren to take immediate and effectual steps for their emancipation.' A copy of this minute was to be sent by the Missionary Secretary to every preacher in the West Indies, with instructions that a report should be given next year as to the way in which it had been observed. Most of the white people who were class-leaders in the West Indies were slave-holders. The missionaries were directed 'to promote the moral and religious improvement of the slaves, without in the least degree, in public or in private, interfering with their civil condition.' The slaves were trained to be patient and faithful without being taught to expect freedom.

The transformation wrought in Jamaica by the ministry of faithful Methodist missionaries was wonderful. ' The savage orgies in which the blacks delighted were abandoned. Methodist hymns took the place of negro songs. The Sunday carnivals, with their riots and obscene processions, became a thing of the past; Sunday markets were abolished; the whole population streamed to worship.' Misrepresentation and calumny were heaped on the missionaries by the slave-holding party, but Richard Watson, the Methodist Missionary Secretary, defended them in a powerful pamphlet which was extensively read by the public men of the day. William Wilberforce greatly appreciated it. It helped to open the eyes of Englishmen to

TABLET TO WILLIAM ARTHUR IN CLAPHAM WESLEYAN CHURCH.

See p. 141.

the ignorance of the slave and the miseries of slavery.

On July 15, 1814, Mr. Thomas Farmer, afterwards Treasurer of the Methodist Missionary Society, describes his attendance at the House of Parliament to present a petition against slavery with more than 36,000 signatures of persons above sixteen years old. The petition was 579 feet long, filled 252 skins of parchment, and weighed 37 lb.

The Methodists put all their strength into the battle for freedom. Out of 352,404 Nonconformist signatures to petitions to Parliament on that behalf 229,426 were those of Methodists. It was a matter of profound thankfulness that during more than seventy years (1760–1834) ' no Methodist slave was ever proved guilty of incendiarism or rebellion.' When the day of liberty, August 1, 1834, approached, the negroes laboured at their tasks till the usual hour of rest on the previous evening, and at ten o'clock streamed to the Methodist chapels. ' A few minutes before midnight

the congregations knelt in silent prayer,
then, as the hour of freedom struck, 800,000
free men poured out their souls in the
doxology :

Praise God, from whom all blessings flow.

Friends and relatives fondly embraced
each other, and returned home thanking
God that they had lived to see the day of
liberty.'

CHAPTER V

THE CHURCH MISSIONARY SOCIETY AND THE BIBLE SOCIETY

With the belief of the inspiration, whether plenary or partial, of the Scriptures, who can reconcile a disbelief of the momentous results with which the mere knowledge of them by mankind at large must be attended ? Who will presume to estimate the workings of such an element of thought in such a world ?—or to follow out the movements resulting from such a voice when raised in every tongue and among all people, in opposition to the rude clamour from without, or the still harsher dissonance from within ?—or who will take on him to measure the consequences of exhibiting amongst all the tribes of men one immutable standard of truth, one eternal rule of duty, one spotless model for imitation ?

SIR JAMES STEPHEN, *The Clapham Sect.*

CHAPTER V

THE CHURCH MISSIONARY SOCIETY AND THE BIBLE SOCIETY

THE Clapham Sect took an active share in the efforts for the spread of gospel truth among the heathen which were one of the glories of their generation. The name of Charles Grant will always have high honour in this respect. He was a Highlander, born at Aldourie Farm on Loch Ness, in March, 1746. He landed in India at the age of twenty-two, and in 1773 entered the service of the East India Company.

Whilst Mr. Charles Grant was serving the East India Company abroad, Dr. Coke, the Methodist missionary pioneer, wrote him in January 1784 as to the ' conversion of the Gentoos to the faith of Christ,' and received a reply dated ' Maldai, February 19, 1785.' He said the fact ' that in the course of twenty years, during which we have possessed extensive territories here, there should have been no public institution for carrying on such work, must doubtless have been matter of regret to many.' Mr. Grant was ready to support a mission if it were 'on principles entirely catholic.' He warned Coke that any mission to India must have ample resources, so that it might not leave its converts who had suffered the loss of all things by becoming Christians to perish for want, or be killed by their kinsmen. Methodism was too much engrossed with its work in the West Indies and in other places to undertake a mission to the East; but in 1805, when the project was taking more definite shape, Coke visited Mr. Grant, then Chairman of the Directors of the East India Company, and was persuaded that though the Company would not consent to a mission for the conversion of the Hindus, it would not prosecute those who might establish such a mission. It was not till the end of 1813 that Coke was able to sail for the East with a band of Methodist missionaries. Mr. Grant entered Parliament in 1802.

In 1793 Wilberforce got a resolution passed in the House of Commons that it was 'the duty of the legislature to adopt such measures as might tend to the advancement of the British Dominions in India in useful knowledge and religious and moral improvement,' and that proper religious provision should be made for the Company's servants. He tried to get a clause inserted in the East India Company's charter sanctioning missionary effort in India, but failed. Successful opposition was made, and from that time missionaries were jealously excluded. But Wilberforce did not lose heart.

In November 1797 he 'dined and slept at Battersea Rise for missionary meeting. Simeon, Charles Grant, Venn. Something, but not much, done. Simeon in earnest.'

At the Eclectic Society, founded by a few clergymen and laymen for the discussion of living questions, on March 18, 1799, John Venn spoke on the question: 'What methods can we use more effectually to promote the knowledge of the gospel among the heathen ? ' He laid down three principles : (1) follow God's leading, and look for success only from the Spirit ; (2) under God, all will depend on the type of men sent forth. A missionary should have heaven in his heart, and tread the world under his feet. And such men only God can raise up ; (3) begin on a small scale.' Mr. Venn deprecated starting with appeals for money. Each member was to admonish his people to promote missions, pray constantly for guidance, study and inquire as to future plans, speak to Christian friends on the subject. The Society was to be founded on 'the Church principle, not the High-Church principle'; and if clergymen could not be found, laymen were to be sent out. Mr. Grant was present. On April 12, 1799, Venn presided over the meeting at which the C.M.S. was founded, at the Castle and Falcon, Aldersgate Street. Wilberforce, Grant, and Samuel Thornton became vice-presidents, Henry Thornton was chosen treasurer, John Venn and C. Elliott were on the committee. Venn drafted the Rules, and as chairman guided the proceedings of the infant society with great wisdom. Money was not lacking. At the first meeting donations of £100 were announced from Wesley's friend, Mr. Wolff, the Danish consul-general, and from Mr. Ambrose Martin, the banker. It was at first called 'the African Institution,' or 'The Society for Missions in Africa and the East.' The title of 'The Church Missionary Society' was not given it till 1812. The Clapham Sect had a peculiar interest in the Society 'because it exactly fitted in with their own favourite project, the abolition of the slave trade.'

In a valedictory address on January 13, 1806, John Venn draws a fine portrait of a true missionary. 'With the world under his feet, with heaven in his eye, with the gospel in his head, and Christ in his heart, he pleads as an ambassador for God, knowing nothing but Jesus Christ, enjoying nothing but the conversion of sinners, hoping for nothing but the promotion of the kingdom of Christ, and glorying in nothing but in the cross of Christ, by which he is crucified to the world and the world to him.' Venn died on July 1, 1813, but, as we shall see, his mantle fell on his son Henry, who was the moving spirit of the Church Missionary Society for thirty years.

For a long time all inquiries for missionaries were fruitless. Henry Martyn was the first Englishman who offered his services. He was a familiar figure at Clapham. It is said that he came 'especially before the people of Clapham because Mr. Grant had brought him on to the Common.' 'Family losses and responsibilities made it impossible for him to take the bare allowance of a missionary ; and beside this, it would have been difficult even for Mr. Grant to obtain leave for his sailing in an East India Company's ship with the direct object of preaching to the heathen.' He was therefore appointed one of the East India Company's chaplains, and sailed for India in 1805. The Committee hoped, after five years' prayer and conference, the appointment might lead to 'considerable influence among the heathen.' The Society turned to Germany. Two students of a missionary seminary in Berlin were accepted as 'missionary catechists,' and were sent to lodge at Clapham at the end of 1802 in order to learn a little English before they sailed. Peter Hartwig evidently made good use of his time, for he married Sarah Windsor, who was governess in John Venn's family. His education in English was thus arranged for ! The accounts of the Society show what was spent on the training of these students and on their passage to Africa with Mrs. Hartwig. Hartwig turned slave-trader, and his wife had to leave him and return home. After several years he 'came to himself,' and his wife rejoined him in Africa, but he died almost immediately, and she returned to England. Three more men from Berlin were sent to South Africa in 1806, but no others were obtained till July 1809.

Zachary Macaulay had taken an active

part in the formation of the Religious Tract Society, and was a member of its committee in 1800. A still nobler society was now to be started on its world-wide course of blessing.

On December 7, 1802, when Thomas Charles of Bala made an appeal to the committee of the Religious Tract Society to assist in supplying the Scriptures in Welsh, Joseph Hughes, the Secretary, who was the Baptist minister in Battersea, spoke the memorable words: 'Surely a society might be formed for the purpose. But if for Wales, why not for the kingdom ? Why not for the world ? ' The proposal was received with enthusiasm ; and by the beginning of 1804, Mr. Canton says, ' the promoters had secured the adhesion of such distinguished men as William Wilberforce, Granville Sharp, Charles Grant, Zachary Macaulay, Lord Teignmouth, and Henry Thornton.' These were all residents at Clapham. On March 7, 1804, Mr. Granville Sharp presided at the meeting at which the British and Foreign Bible Society was founded. Mr. Henry Thornton was

appointed treasurer, and on May 16 Lord
Teignmouth became the first president.

Sir John Shore, better known as Lord
Teignmouth, was one of the most distinguished yet most modest of the 'great Claphamites.' He sprang from the Shores of
Snitterton Hall near Matlock, but was born
in London in 1751 and educated at Harrow
and at a commercial school in Hackney
for the service of the East India Company.
His father was a supercargo in the same
service, and his grandfather a captain in the
Company's Marine.

When John Shore was nineteen the in-
dolence of his chief and the absence of the
second officer in authority led to his being
suddenly invested with civil and fiscal
jurisdiction over a large district at Moor-
shedabad. An old gentleman called Burgess
had given him some golden advice : ' Make
yourself useful, and you will succeed.'
John Shore acted on that wise hint. Every
opportunity of distinction found him ready.
He learned Hindustani, Arabic, and
Persian, and was summoned to use his

knowledge as a member of the Provincial Council at Calcutta. Warren Hastings warmly recognized his ability and fidelity.

They returned to England together in June 1785. Shore's friends were few, and he had only one relative—a brother who had recently married W. Mackworth Praed's daughter and was staying at her father's house near Exeter. The lonely Indian official went down to Devonshire unexpectedly. His brother and his wife were from home, but a young lady of great personal attractions, who had been detained at the house by a snowstorm, received him. 'In their first interview Shore's ' affections became so much engaged that he sought fresh opportunities of cultivating her acquaintance.' She was the only daughter of a widow, Mrs. Cornish, whose husband had been collector of customs at Teignmouth. Shore married Miss Charlotte Cornish on February 14, 1786. Forty-two years later he told his son, ' I could very conscientiously claim the flitch of bacon at Dunmow.'

Pitt had his eye on his brother-in-law, the Hon. Edward Eliot, as Viceroy of India, and when family affliction made that impossible, he turned to Mr. Shore. Burke was in arms against the appointment of one who had been closely associated with Hastings, but the Directors declared their absolute confidence in his uprightness.

On September 15, 1792, Wilberforce says: 'At Mr. Grant's persuasion returned to Clapham for the purpose of seeing Shore (who is just appointed Governor-General) and instituting a connexion with him for the sake of Indian subjects.' Wilberforce saw a good deal of Sir John, and was 'much pleased with him.' He tells us that Shore's reluctance to accept the great post was so strong that Pitt induced Mr. Charles Grant to visit him and urge him to make this sacrifice in consideration of the eminent service he could render.

Mr. Shore was created a baronet. He was Viceroy from 1793 to 1798. An entry in his journal shows the spirit in which he took up his great office: 'Grant, I beseech Thee, that I may on all occasions regulate my conduct by the rules and precepts of Thy Word ; and that in all doubts, dangers, and embarrassments, I may always have grace to apply to Thee for support and assistance. Grant that under my government, religion and morality may be advanced.' He does not rank among the great rulers of India, but no more pure or more upright man ever occupied that proud position. Sir James Stephen speaks of his rule as ' barren and temporizing and timid.' It must be added, however, that he ' faithfully obeyed his instructions. Nothing more could be expected of him.' [1]

When his successor was appointed Sir John was raised to the peerage, and retired to Clapham in August 1802, in order to be near the Grants, Wilberforce, and Thornton. He lived in old John Thornton's house, which he had taken from Samuel Thornton, M.P., who removed to Albury Park. It had a small estate attached, and a farm of twenty-two acres.

[1] *Dictionary of National Biography.*

There he prepared, at the widow's request,
the Memoirs of his friend, Sir William Jones,
the great Indian scholar. The dedication
to Lady Jones is dated 'Clapham, June 20,
1804.'

Many were disappointed when they first
saw 'the mild old gentleman, with his
phlegmatic manner and somewhat inex-
pressive countenance, who seated himself
in a corner of the Clapham coach, with his
umbrella by his side,' and were told that
this unassuming man had been Governor-
General of India.

Lord Teignmouth was connected with
the Bible Society for thirty years. Bishop
Porteus suggested his name as that of one
singularly fitted for the office of President
in 1804. He gave unremitting attention
to the work, writing the earlier reports and
presiding at every anniversary save one
until 1831. That year the meeting was in
Wesley's Chapel, City Road, and ladies were
admitted for the first time. Lord Teignmouth was not well enough to be present.
His son speaks of the host of visitors who

came to his father's house at Clapham. A celebrated Mohawk chief spent some weeks under this hospitable roof, while he was translating St. Matthew's Gospel into the language of his people. He used to delight the young folk of the family by performing his war dance.

When Napoleon formed his military camp at Boulogne in 1803, England was filled with patriotic fervour. Lord Teignmouth undertook the Lieutenancy of Surrey. His son remembered Zachary Macaulay marching at the head of a company of Clapham volunteers with a bearskin-covered helmet, and Charles and Robert Grant as ' extemporized dragoons.'

In 1807 Lord Teignmouth let his house for some months to Mr. Perceval, then Chancellor of the Exchequer. He spent the summer and autumn with his family at Broadstairs. They returned to Clapham in December, but on July 23, 1808, moved to Portman Square. They had taken special interest in a large district in the vicinity of their house at Clapham, and continued to visit it after their removal to London. When they left Clapham 'the sorrow expressed by the multitude of persons who covered the lawn in the front of the house, and crowded along the roadside to bid them farewell, bore feeling testimony to the affection and gratitude with which they had been regarded.'

Lord Teignmouth felt that it would be hard to find such a pastor as John Venn in his new neighbourhood. He tells Wilberforce: 'I certainly feel more than I can express at quitting a place where I enjoyed all the comforts this world can afford, during seven years.'

Sir James Stephen says: 'There was blended in Lord Teignmouth as much of the spirit of the world, and as much of the spirit of that sacred volume, as could combine harmoniously with each other.' For many years he spent three hours a day in private prayer. He used to retire for this purpose at five in order that he might not be too weary for his devotions. On the last Sunday of his life he said to his wife and children: 'I feel that I am resting upon the right foundation, and I can now leave you all rejoicing.' He died at his house, 4 Portman Square, on February 14, 1834, and was buried in Marylebone parish church, where a monument is erected to his memory. It describes him as 'President of the British and Foreign Bible Society, from its foundation to his death, a period of thirty years, and formerly Governor-General of India.' His wife died four months after him.

The two elder sons of John Thornton, who divided his estate on the south side of the Common between them, were Robert Thornton, M.P. for Colchester, and Samuel Thornton, M.P. for Surrey and Governor of the Bank of England. Samuel Thornton entertained Pitt and most of his Cabinet at dinner at Clapham in 1800. The banquet was given in the summer-house of his brother Robert, which was fitted up for the occasion. It is still to be seen in the grounds of the Catholic nunnery. Robert Thornton lived next door to his brother Samuel. His American and Dutch gardens were famous, and formed a leading attraction of his garden-parties, which the great folk of London frequented. Mr. Thornton's fortune was dissipated in this way, and he spent his last years in the United States. Samuel Thornton purchased Albury Park, near Guildford, but when involved in business troubles, through the French war in 1810, that estate was sold to Mr. Drummond, with whose daughter it passed to the Duke of Northumberland.

Henry Thornton had always been delicate, but in October 1814 grave symptoms of consumption developed, and he was moved from his house in Palace Yard to Wilberforce's home in Kensington Gore, where every loving attention was shown him. He died in calm and patient hope on January 16, 1815. He was born in 1760. Zachary Macaulay wrote to the widow: 'I can truly say that for the last twenty-two years he was, as it were, my polar-star, my presiding, my better genius. A thought of him, of the gleam of his approbation, or of his graver look of doubt or dissent, mingled itself insensibly, not merely with my larger pursuits, my plans and schemes in life, but with almost all I wrote or did. What will Henry Thornton say ? was with me a trying question on all occasions.' He adds : ' I have been pleasing myself with figuring to my mind our dear friend Venn welcoming his former associate in the heavenly course to a participation of the joys with a foretaste of which they had been blessed on earth.'

Mrs. Thornton also died of consumption at Brighton in the following October. Zachary Macaulay visited her there, and arranged all her affairs. He and her brother, Daniel Sykes, were her executors, Charles and Robert Grant were the guardians of her sons, Mr. and Mrs. Robert Inglis of her daughters. Wilberforce stood by her death-bed. The body was brought to Battersea Rise on October 18, and next day laid beside that of her husband. Zachary Macaulay wrote : ' It is impossible to imagine a death more truly consolatory

THE THORNTON TOMB, AND HENRY THORNTON'S TABLET.

and even beautiful. Her repose not only of mind but of body seemed hardly to be disturbed for an instant; and the nearer she drew to the horizon, the more clear and cloudless appeared her prospect. It was perfect peace, the peace which passeth understanding.'

The golden age of 'the villa-cinctured Common' was perhaps from 1800 to 1820. Wilberforce gave up his home at Broomfield with deep regret in 1808. John Venn died in July 1813.

Before Mr. and Mrs. Thornton died, the Grants, Stephens, and Teignmouths had gone to different parts of London, and in 1818 the Macaulays moved to Cadogan Place, where they were near to Wilberforce at Kensington Gore.

But if the Sect severed its connexion with Clapham it pursued those great objects of religion and philanthropy which have won for it enduring honour. On May 8, 1819, Zachary Macaulay tells Hannah More: 'At the meeting of the Bible Society, Wilberforce was exquisite. Age, instead of damping the wings of his imagination, seems to have lent them new elasticity. It was the expansion and elevation of a spirit freed from its corporeal trammels and mundane feelings; and while it exulted itself in the goodness of God, and in the opening prospects of the Saviour's kingdom, communicated to every other spirit a sympathetic flow of spiritual affection and heavenly aspiration. His very countenance seemed irradiated with the light of heaven, and his voice spoke in every tone its accents.'

Wilberforce visited Clapham in 1830. He says: 'We are spending a little time at this to me deeply interesting place. I always visit the funeral urn—H. T., January 16, 1815. M. T., October 12, 1815.'

Some other names deserve mention. William Smith, M.P. for Norwich, the grandfather of Florence Nightingale, lived at Clapham in the first years of the nineteenth century, and was very intimate with Zachary Macaulay. He was a Unitarian and a strong abolitionist. 'He lived as

if to show how much of the coarser duties
of this busy world may be undertaken by
a man of quick sensibility, without im-
pairing the finer sense of the beautiful in
nature and in art ; and as if to prove how
much a man of ardent benevolence may
enjoy of this world's happiness, without
any steeling of the heart to the wants and
calamities of others.'

A worker not less noble than Wilberforce
and Thornton claims a passing word. At
Maisonette, near Battersea Rise, lived Sir
James Mackintosh, the jurist and philo-
sopher who secured the abolition of capital
punishment for such offences as sheep-
stealing and forgery. Wilberforce visited
him here in 1830, and says, ' He is at
everybody's service, and his conversation
is always rich and sparkling.'

A man of another type, Henry Cavendish, ' the Newton of chemistry,' lived on
the south side of the Common, where he
buried himself from the world to pursue
his researches into the composition of water
and the density of the earth. He is de-

scribed as 'the man who weighed the world.'

He died at Cavendish House in 1810, leaving a million of money to be divided among his relatives. The man who had £80,000 lying to his credit at his banker's and threatened to remove the account if he was disturbed about so small a matter, is not the least interesting figure of Clapham Common. He had an immense library, and his house was filled with all manner of scientific instruments. His housekeeper once reminded him that five friends were coming to dinner, and one leg of mutton would not be enough. 'Well, then, have two,' was the answer.

The abolition of the slave trade was the peculiar glory of the Clapham Sect. Thomas Clarkson had rendered yeoman service to the cause, and many had helped nobly. 'But, making every allowance for the services which others rendered, it must still be admitted that Wilberforce, aided by his Clapham friends Thornton and Macaulay and Stephen, was the real mainspring of the movement ; and if the Clapham Sect had done nothing else, this work alone would have rendered that body immortal. But they did very much else. It was very largely through their influence that the Church Missionary Society was founded and placed upon the excellent business footing which it has always since maintained. Little as well as great ways of doing good received their effective support. " Schools, prison discipline, savings-banks, tracts, village libraries, district visitings, and church buildings, each for a time rivalled their cosmopolitan projects. Every human interest had its guardian, every region of the globe its representative." ' [1]

[1] Overton and Relton, *History of the English Church*, 1714–1800, p. 234.

CHAPTER VI

THE INHERITORS OF THE GREAT TRADITION

How do I feel more than requited for all the pains I have taken, and the prayers I have offered, when I read your earnest desires that you may glorify God! Supernatural is that desire; it is the bud and the blossom, which bring forth all the fruit the Church of God bears. . . . This supreme desire to glorify God is like a friendly clue in a labyrinth, which guides us out of all perplexities, and excites an earnest cry, which, in time, brings us to the enjoyment of our God and Saviour, gives us increasing views of His excellency and glory, and ripens us for the vast assembly of perfect spirits, who are swallowed up in love and adoration of God, and are perfectly one with each other.

HENRY VENN to one of his children, 1785.

CHAPTER VI

THE INHERITORS OF THE GREAT TRADITION

THE members of the Clapham Sect did a work in their own generation the influence of which is still felt throughout the world of philanthropy and religion. Yet amid their unwearying service for the slave and the heathen they never ceased to cultivate 'domestic affection and family piety.' How well they laid the foundations is shown by the lives of their children. There was no lack of gifts and eloquence and literary skill in the next generation, and the way in which these were consecrated to the service of God and man showed that the sons and daughters were worthy to take their place beside such fathers as William Wilberforce, Zachary Macaulay, Henry Thornton, Charles Grant, James Stephen, and Lord Teignmouth.

One looks on those lovely families with pride and thankfulness. In the parish church of Clapham a century ago, Wilberforces, Thorntons, Macaulays, Stephens sat in adjacent pews ; the Teignmouths had a seat in the front gallery. One of the children who sat there, Sir James Stephen, bears witness that the religion taught in the homes of the Clapham Sect was 'a hardy, serviceable, fruit-bearing, patrimonial religion.' There was no one in that band of workers for the uplifting of the world who was not most keenly solicitous for the spiritual good of his own children, and would not have felt that failure to lead them in the right way would have been dearly bought at the cost of success of any other kind.

After the death of John Venn, in 1813, the parish was fortunate enough to secure Dr. Dealtry as his successor. He had been Second Wrangler in 1796, and was Fellow and Tutor of Trinity College. He was a man of generous instincts, and deserves special recognition as one of the earliest friends of Henry Kirke White.

He was doing duty at Clapham at the time of Mr. Venn's death, and young and old cried out for his appointment. He was a singularly persuasive preacher. A lady of Clapham described him as 'the ugly little brown bird who sang so sweetly.' No man was better fitted to enlist the sympathy and guide the lives of the rising youth of Clapham House. He held the rectory till his death in 1847, at the age of seventy-two. John Thornton, Jun., wrote the inscription on his tablet in the parish church, and the Rev. A. R. Pennington, sometime Rector of Utterby, says: 'I can bear witness to the truth of every word of it.'

The pulpit at Clapham was worthy of its office, and it was nobly supported by the home life of the best families around the Common. The mode of education among them was 'simple, without being severe. In the spacious gardens, and the commodious houses of an architecture already dating a century back, which surrounded the Common, there was plenty of freedom and good fellowship, and reasonable enjoyment for young and old alike. There can have been nothing that was vulgar, and little that was narrow, in a training which produced Samuel Wilberforce, Sir James Stephen, Charles and Robert Grant, and Lord Macaulay. The plan on which children were brought up in the chosen home of the Low Church party during its golden age will bear comparison with systems about which in their day the world was supposed never to tire of hearing, although their ultimate results have been small indeed.'

Mr. G. W. E. Russell, who was ' brought up among the spiritual descendants of the men and women who constituted the Clapham Sect, and attended Henry Drummond's Prophetical Conferences at Albury,' gives a beautiful account of ' Evangelical training in the home.' [1] First the children were taught the gospel plan of salvation, and shown that conversion was the acceptance of the offer of salvation. They were instructed in the Bible from their earliest

[1] *The Household of Faith*, pp. 239-44.

years. Adam Clarke's Commentary was one of their helps to its study. ' Hymns played a great part in our training. As soon as we could speak we learned " When rising from the bed of death," and " Beautiful Zion, built above " ; " Rock of Ages," and " Jesu, Lover of my soul," were soon added.'

Mr. Russell gives a sketch of the happy arts by which the young folk of such circles were started on the path of service. ' While we were still very young children, we were carefully incited to acts of practical charity. We began by carrying dinners to the sick and aged poor ; then we went on to reading hymns and bits of the Bible to the blind and unlettered. As soon as we were old enough, we became teachers in Sunday schools, and conducted classes and cottage meetings. From the very beginning we were taught to save up our money for good causes. Each of us had a " missionary box," and I remember another box, in the counterfeit presentment of a Gothic church, which received contributions for the Church Pastoral Aid Society.

'An aunt of mine, bursting into unlooked-for melody, wrote for the benefit of her young relations :

Would you like to be told the best use of a penny ?
I can tell you a use which is better than any—
Not on toys, nor on fruit, nor on sweetmeats to
    spend it,
But over the seas to the heathen to send it.

Mr. Russell adds, ' The constructive part of my early teaching has always been, and is, the bed-rock of my religious life ; but as time went on the negative dialectics seemed to wear a little thin.'

The children of these homes were taught not less by example than by precept. They saw those whom they loved and honoured spending their strength for the poor and oppressed. The homes of Wilberforce and Zachary Macaulay were temples of industry. ' It is easy,' says Sir G. O. Trevelyan, ' to trace whence the great bishop and the great writer derived their immense industry. Working came as naturally as walking to sons who could not remember a time when their fathers idled.' ' Mr. Wilberforce and

Mr. Babington have never appeared down-
stairs lately, except to take a hasty dinner,
and for half an hour after we have supped.
The slave trade now occupies them nine
hours daily. They talk of sitting up one
night in every week to do their work.'[1]

No toiler in all the company was more
indefatigable than Zachary Macaulay.
'That God had called him into being to
wage war with this gigantic evil [of the
slave trade] became his immutable con-
viction. During forty successive years he
was ever burdened with the thought. In
that service he sacrificed all that a man
may lawfully sacrifice—health, fortune, repose, favour, celebrity.'[2]

The two sandy-haired Grants sat with
their father in the pew before the Penningtons in Clapham Parish Church. In
1801, when Henry Martyn was Senior
Wrangler, Charles Grant was First Classical Medallist and Fourth Wrangler, and
his brother Robert was Second Classical

[1] *Life of Macaulay* i. 64.
[2] *Ibid.* p. 65.

Medallist and Third Wrangler. Charles
Grant became Secretary for Ireland and
Secretary for the Colonies, and was made
a peer. His title 'Glenelg' spells exactly
the same both ways, so that he was known
as 'Lord Backwards and Forwards.' Lack
of energy robbed him of the great position
that seemed opening before him, but he
was a graceful and eloquent speaker.

The younger brother is better known
to this generation.

At the Bible Society meeting in 1820,
Zachary Macaulay says : ' Robert Grant
made one of his powerful displays. It
was even sublime in some parts, but it
was too ethereal for common minds, and
it also came too late in the day. Brilliant
as he was, some brutal persons at the
extremity of the room became impatient,
and he was actually coughed down. It
was most provoking, but what human
enjoyment is without its alloy ? It was
a mistake to call up one who had so much
to say, and could say it so well, at half-past
four o'clock, when the meeting was ex-

GLENELG.

hausted partly by excitement, and partly by having been many of them shut up in the hall for seven or eight hours.'

Robert Grant became Governor of Bombay, but his chief title to remembrance is his hymns, 'Saviour, when in dust to Thee,' 'When gathering clouds around I view,' 'O worship the King, all glorious above,' which are still dear to every section of the Christian Church.

Samuel Wilberforce, the third son of William Wilberforce, was born at Broomfield on September 7, 1805, in a first-floor room with bow windows which looked to the north. His father took a vigilant interest in his training. Some six hundred of his letters to Samuel still remain. Canon Ashwell says: 'Nascent faults carefully marked and checked, personal habits of upright conduct strenuously enforced, shrewd practical counsels as to social duties and conduct toward his equals constantly suggested, and all these strung upon the one thread of private prayer as the only hold-fast of life. These remarkable letters exhibit the influence which formed that solid substratum of character which underlay the brilliant gifts and the striking career of Samuel Wilberforce.' His father trained him to speak freely without notes on a subject with which he had made himself well acquainted, and to trust to the inspiration of the moment for suitable words. To this he largely owed his facility of speech. Wilberforce became the most popular speaker and preacher in the Church of England. Dean Burgon says that ' as a public man, Samuel Wilberforce, by the general suffrage of English Society, was without a peer.' His faults were patent. He was ' too facile,' and was sometimes betrayed into unwise and ill-judged words and actions. He had little of the saving grace of caution, but, whatever his faults, he was true to the teaching of the Clapham Sect. He was a noble evangelical preacher.

Thomas Babington Macaulay eclipses all his Clapham contemporaries by the lustre of his gifts as orator and historian. He was

born on October 25, 1800, and brought to
Clapham when he was a child of two. The
Macaulays' house, now No. 5, The Pavement, was roomy and comfortable, with a
very small garden behind and a tiny one in
front. From the time Macaulay was three
years old he used to read incessantly, lying
for the most part before the fire with his
book on the ground and a piece of bread-and
butter in his hand. 'A very clever woman
who then lived in the house as parlourmaid
told how he used to sit in his nankeen
frock, perched on the table by her as she
was cleaning the plate, and expounding
to her out of a volume as big as himself.'

Macaulay's nephew and biographer, Sir
G. O. Trevelyan, says (*Life*, i. pp. 28-9) :
'He had at his command the resources
of the Common—to this day the most
unchanged spot within ten miles of St.
Paul's, and which to all appearance will
ere long hold that pleasant pre-eminence
within ten leagues. That delightful wilder-
ness of gorse-bushes, and poplar groves,
and gravel-pits, and ponds great and

small, was to little Tom Macaulay a region of inexhaustible romance and mystery. He explored its recesses ; he composed, and almost believed, its legends ; he invented for its different features a nomenclature which has been faithfully preserved by two generations of children. A slight ridge intersected by deep ditches towards the west of the Common, the very existence of which no one above eight years old would notice, was dignified with the title of the Alps ; while the elevated island, covered with shrubs, that gives a name to the Mount pool, was regarded with infinite awe as being the nearest approach within the circuit of his observation to a conception of the majesty of Sinai. Indeed at this period his infant fancy was much exercised with the threats and terrors of the Law. He had a little plot of ground at the back of the house, marked out as his own by a row of oyster-shells which a maid one day threw away as rubbish. He went straight to the drawing-room, where his mother was entertaining some visitors, walked into the circle, and said very solemnly : " Cursed be Sally ; for it is written, ' Cursed is he that removeth his neighbour's land-mark.' "

' A more simple and natural child never lived, or a more lively and merry one.' As a small child he went reluctantly to the school kept by William Greaves, the master who had been brought to Clapham to train the West African children. When the climate proved fatal to them, the children of the residents round the Common were sent to the school.

The second Lord Teignmouth, born at Calcutta in 1796, was the first Clapham scholar sent to Mr. Greaves. There were then about six negro youths of good family, [1] ' older than myself and very good-natured.' For the first month, till the Wilberforces, Stephens, Thorntons, and others came, he studied with the black boys. ' On one occasion they showed that they had not unlearnt their native superstitions ; for on a black dog belonging to

[1] *Reminiscences of Many Years*, 1878.

Mr. Greaves uttering a peculiar bark, they rushed in a body down to the kitchen, from whence it was no easy task to dislodge them.' Two of the black boys remained for some time in the school.

Greaves was a portly, good-natured man. ' Some years after he had given up tuition, several of us invited ourselves to dine with him under the old roof as a spontaneous token of our feelings, which much gratified him.'

Besides Macaulay, Samuel Wilberforce and the future Bishop Perry of Melbourne were pupils here. Greaves was a shrewd Yorkshireman with a turn for science. The schoolroom was a good-sized apartment on the first floor, lofty and with an arched ceiling. The cupboards where the scholars kept their books still remain. Macaulay had his best teachers in his father's library. Long afterwards he speaks of ' a translation of some Spanish comedies, one of the very few bright specks in our very sullen library at Clapham.' His mother wrote in September 1808 : ' My dear Tom continues to show marks of uncommon genius.

He gets on wonderfully in all branches of his education, and the extent of his reading, and of the knowledge he has derived from it, are truly astonishing in a boy not yet eight years old. He is at the same time as playful as a kitten.' A year earlier he had written a compendium of Universal History, and had drawn up a paper which was to be translated into Malabar to persuade the people of Travancore to accept Christianity. Scott had already fired his martial imagination, and he had begun a poem on the 'Battle of Cheviot.' He had also written many hymns.

Miss Fanny Macaulay, the only surviving sister, lodged in the schoolhouse in 1855. Mr. Stroud's school, where Tom Hood was educated, was at Clarence House.

Lady Trevelyan writes of her early life at Clapham : ' I think that my father's strictness was a good counterpoise to the perfect worship of your uncle by the rest of the family. To us he was an object of passionate love and devotion. To us he could do no wrong. His unruffled sweetness of

temper, his unfailing flow of spirits, his
amusing talk, all made his presence delightful, so that his wishes and his tastes were
our law. He hated strangers, and his
notion of perfect happiness was to see us
all working round him while he read aloud
a novel, and then to walk all together on
the Common, or, if it rained, to have a
frightfully noisy game of hide-and-seek.'

Macaulay's bedroom was the front room
of the top story, on the side nearest
London. There he made his first venture
in literature by preparing the index to the
thirteenth volume of the *Christian Observer*
during his Christmas holiday of 1814.

One local personage of those days left
an abiding impression on the mind of Lord
Macaulay and his sisters. She was a
Baptist schoolmistress who lived close to
Clapham Town. 'The house, with its charm-
ing grounds, has recently been incorporated
with the block of convent schools and other
monastic buildings which occupy a large
area on the western side of the Common.'
Zachary Macaulay says she is 'rather in

high esteem among our religious folks at Clapham, who are moved by her active benevolence to recede a little from their accustomed antipathy to Dissenters.' She invited a Church of England charity school to a feast with her own school one year and gave them plain pudding, whilst her own children had beef and plum pudding. She grew more generous by-and-by, for when *Zachary Macaulay* went to the feast on June 4, 1799, he says, ' She avoided this fault yesterday, however.' Lord Macaulay remembered the horror with which he and his sisters watched the schoolmistress knitting at her window when they came out of church on Christmas morning. Her dinner that day was roast veal and apple pie instead of the customary beef and plum pudding.

From Clapham Macaulay went as a pupil to the Rev. Mr. Preston, at Little Shelford, near Cambridge. He tells his father that he is classed with Wilberforce, the eldest son, ' whom all the boys allow to be very clever, very droll, and very impudent.' The boys had just started a debating society. 'A vote of censure was moved for upon Wilberforce, but he, getting up, said, " Mr. President, I beg to second the motion." By this means he escaped.'

Mrs. Macaulay wrote to her boy from Clapham, May 28 :

'MY DEAR TOM,—I am very happy to hear that you have so far advanced in your different prize exercises, and with such little fatigue. I know you write with great ease to yourself, and would rather write ten poems than prune one ; but remember that excellence is not obtained at first. All your pieces are much mended after a little reflection, and therefore take some solitary walks, and think over each separate thing. Spare no time or trouble to make each piece as perfect as you can, and then leave the event without one anxious thought. I have always admired a saying of one of the old heathen philosophers. When a friend was condoling with him that he deserved so well of the gods, and yet that they did not shower their favours on him, as on some others less worthy, he answered, " I will, however, continue to deserve well of them." So do you, my dearest. Do your best because it is the will of God you should improve every faculty to the utmost now, and strengthen the powers of your mind by exercise, and then in future you will be better enabled to glorify God with all your powers and talents, be they of a more humble, or higher order, and you shall not fail to be received into everlasting habitations, with the applauding voice of your Saviour, " Well done, good and faithful servant." You see how ambitious your mother is. She must have the wisdom of her son acknowledged before angels and an assembled world. My wishes can soar no higher, and they can be content with nothing less for any of my children. The first time I saw your face, I repeated those beautiful lines of Watts's cradle hymn—

> Mayst thou live to know and fear Him,
> Trust and love Him all thy days,
> *Then* go dwell for ever near Him,
> See His face, and sing His praise.

'And this is the substance of all my prayers for you. In less than a month you and I shall, I trust, be rambling over the Common, which now looks quite beautiful.

'I am ever, my dear Tom,

'Your affectionate mother,

'SELINA MACAULAY.'

Zachary Macaulay tried to lead his children to that loving care for others which was his own glory. In 1814, when the schoolboy complained of the people of Shelford, his father reminded him that the best thing which he and his schoolfellows could do would be to try to reform them. 'You can buy and distribute useful and striking tracts, as well as Testaments, among such as can read. The cheap Repository and Religious Tract Society will furnish tracts suited to all descriptions of persons; and for those who cannot read— why should you not institute a Sunday-school to be taught by yourselves, and in which, appropriate rewards being given for good behaviour, not only at school but throughout the week, great effects of a moral kind might soon be produced.'

The family moved to Cadogan Place in 1818, where they set up a larger establishment. Zachary Macaulay believed himself to be worth a hundred thousand pounds. In 1823 financial circumstances had become threatening, and they removed to 50 Great Ormond Street.

Macaulay went up to Trinity College, Cambridge, in October 1818. ' Of all his places of sojourn during his joyous and shining pilgrimage through the world, Trinity, and Trinity alone, had any share with his home in Macaulay's affection and loyalty.' Mr. H. S. Thornton was his banker, and, says Macaulay, had ' as sound a judgement in money matters as I ever met with. You might have safely followed him blindfold.'

In June 1824 Macaulay spoke at a meeting of the Anti-Slavery Society, over which the Duke of Gloucester presided at Freemasons' Tavern. The *Edinburgh*

Review says it was 'a display of eloquence so signal for rare and matured excellence that the most practised orator may well admire how it should have come from one who then for the first time addressed a public assembly.'   Sir G. O. Trevelyan says : 'That was probably the happiest half-hour of Zachary Macaulay's life.'   He sat with his eyes fixed on a piece of paper, and only referred to the speech that evening to say that it was ungraceful in so young a man to speak with folded arms in the presence of royalty.   Wilberforce said : 'My friend would doubtless willingly bear with all the base falsehoods, all the vile calumnies, all the detestable artifices which have been aimed against him, to render him the martyr and victim of our cause, for the gratification he has this day enjoyed in hearing one so dear to him plead such a cause in such a manner.'

Macaulay never ceased to love Clapham. When he revisited the old home in the High Street, 'though he had not been in it for sixteen years he remembered the locks on

CLAPHAM WESLEYAN CHURCH.

the doors.' He went over the church in February 1849, and said, 'I love the church for the sake of old times.'

On July 5, 1858, Macaulay writes: 'Motley called. I like him much. We agree wonderfully well about slavery, and it is not often that I meet any person with whom I agree on that subject. For I hate slavery from the bottom of my soul; and yet I am made sick by the cant and the silly mock reasons of the Abolitionists. The nigger-driver and the negrophile are two odious things to me.'

The extraordinary success of his *History of England* was the crown of Macaulay's reputation. He was made a baron in 1857. He died suddenly on December 28, 1859, and was buried in Westminster Abbey at the foot of Addison's statue in Poet's Corner, with the proud words engraved on the slab:

> His body is buried in peace,
> But his name liveth for evermore.

After the death of Mr. and Mrs. Thornton,

Mr. R. Inglis and his wife came to Battersea
Rise and took charge of the nine orphans.
We get some pleasant glimpses of them
in the letters of Zachary Macaulay. In
January 1816 he says : 'The Inglises are
very good, and very amiable, and very
well bred, and they have also very good
sense and a great deal of heart. They are
delighted w'.h their charge and their
occupations, and seem thoroughly comfortable.' Two years later Mr. Macaulay
describes them as the kindest people he
ever knew. 'True kindness, gentleness,
courtesy, everything that can flow from
genuine and undissembled Christian affection
and Christian humility in union, distinguish
them in a very marked degree.'

Sir Hugh Inglis was chairman of the
East India Company in 1813. On his
death in 1820 his son Robert succeeded to
the baronetcy, and in 1829 followed Peel
as member for Oxford University. He
served in nine parliaments. In his day
Battersea Rise was the 'resort of every
man of note or genius, who either dwelt in

London or visited it.' Southey first met Wilberforce there in 1817, and Sir Walter Scott also visited Battersea Rise. Sir Robert was a great traveller, who rolled along the roads of Europe in his yellow chariot scattering small coins among the beggars 'because it made the poor creatures look so happy.' He moved from Clapham to Bedford Square in 1833.

Henry Thornton's nephew John, who had been made a member of the Bible Society's Committee in 1805, succeeded his uncle as Treasurer. He was in his thirty-second year, and held the office for thirty-seven years. At Cambridge he had been the intimate friend of Reginald Heber and the Grants, and Heber visited him at Clapham. John Thornton, Jun., was President of the North India Bible Society at Benares in 1844. Edward N. Thornton was for forty years, 1809–48, a member of the Committee.

Henry Sykes Thornton, the eldest son of Mr. Henry Thornton, M.P., entered Trinity College, Cambridge, in October

1818, at the same time as T. B. Macaulay. They shared the same lodgings in Jesus Lane and read with the same tutor. But as Macaulay did not love mathematics and was always arguing about them, his friend found it necessary to break through this arrangement. He got a Trinity Scholarship with T. B. Macaulay in the spring of 1820. He was Fourth Wrangler of his year, and on the advice of his uncle, Daniel Sykes, Esq., F.R.S., M.P. for Hull, gave up his prospect of a Trinity Fellowship to take his place as a banker in the City. After the crash of 1825 he reconstituted the firm of Thornton & Free and gradually built up a great reputation as head of the banking house of Williams, Deacon & Co. He died suddenly in his eighty-second year, and on the day of his funeral all the busmen between the City and Clapham wore black rosettes as a tribute to one whose kindly greeting they had prized for many years.

Marianne Thornton's extraordinary tenderness and fortitude at the time of her father's and mother's death in 1815 made a profound impression on Zachary Macaulay, who says, 'Her character for sense and piety rises higher as one knows her better.' Mr. G. W. E. Russell speaks of her as 'the truly venerable lady through whom I am myself linked to the earlier Evangelicals, and to the Clapham Sect.' She was the last survivor of the generation to which Lord Macaulay and Sir Robert Grant belonged, and of the Clapham Sect. Bishop Wilberforce greatly esteemed her, and their correspondence with each other was kept up to the end of his life. She died at her house near the fire-escape station and opposite to the pond close to Clapham Church. Her tablet in the parish church reads :

In Memory of
MARIANNE THORNTON
Born March 10, 1797
Died November 5, 1887.

———

'She opened her mouth with wisdom.'

Henry Venn, son of John Venn, and Secretary of the C.M.S., was born at Clapham Rectory, on February 10, 1796.

In 1805 he and Samuel Thornton, son of Mr. Samuel Thornton, M.P. for Surrey, and father of Mr. Percy M. Thornton, M.P., were pupils under his father at the Rectory ; but ill-health and pressure of other work only allowed John Venn to spare them an hour in the morning. The boys used to spend their holidays together at Albury Park, where Samuel Thornton's father lived. Young Thornton went to sea in 1814. His coach was late at Portsmouth, so that he missed being on board the *Shannon* in her fight with the *Chesapeake*. He did not lack compensation, for he was taken on the *Phoebe*, which captured the *Essex*, an American frigate, in Valparaiso Bay that year. Henry Venn was only seventeen when his father died, but he was left as one of the executors of his father's will with this tribute : ' His prudence and discretion will amply make up for his want of years and experience.' He was Nineteenth Wrangler in 1818, and became, like his grandfather, a Fellow of Queens'. On June 19, 1820, Z. Macaulay tells Hannah More : ' I heard Henry Venn (our dear friend Venn's eldest son) preach yesterday for the first time. It was a sermon of great power and still greater promise. It is delightful to see a fourth generation of Venns thus taking their stand on the Lord's side. The second son goes out to India in a few weeks with higher honours on his head, both literary and moral, than any young man has yet carried away from the East India College.' In 1821 Venn was curate at St. Dunstan's, Fleet Street, and began to attend the Committee of the C.M.S. Then he returned to Cambridge as Tutor at his college. Wilberforce nominated him Vicar of Drypool in Hull. He married in 1829 Martha, fourth daughter of Nicholas Sykes of Swanland (Yorks), a niece of Mrs. Henry Thornton. In 1834 he took the incumbency of St. John's, Holloway, and in 1841 began his thirty-one years of priceless service as Hon. Secretary of the C.M.S.

Henry Venn's ' great wish was to die in harness, and he greatly envied the

13

departure of one of his chief friends, a
Secretary of the Wesleyan Methodists
(Rev. Dr. Beecham) who, with a sharp and
sudden transition, had been called from
his labour to his rest.' He quietly passed
away on January 13, 1873, and was buried
in Mortlake Cemetery. Samuel Wilberforce, who had been baptized by his father,
wrote : ' You must look on his life as a
grand epic poem which has ended in an
euthanasia of victory and rest.' He told
Miss M. Thornton, January 14, 1873 : ' Once
or twice, through the *Record* and otherwise,
Venn has smitten me hard when he thought
I in any way wronged the C.M.S., but I
no more resented it than I should have
resented Sir Lancelot's chivalry for his
queen.'

John Venn's second daughter, Jane
Catherine, married (Sir) James Stephen in
1814. Sir James Fitz-James Stephen and
Sir Leslie Stephen were her sons. Leslie
Stephen wrote : ' I have never seen one like
her to my thinking, and I suppose I never
shall.'

The *Greville Memoirs*, in 1833, refer to the fact that Stephen had resigned £3,000 a year at the Bar and taken £1,500 at the Colonial Office, principally in order to advance the cause of emancipation. He ' owned that he had never known so great a problem, nor so difficult a question to settle. If the sentiments of justice and benevolence with which he is actuated were common to all who profess the same opinions, or if the same sagacity and resource which he possesses were likely to be applied to the practical operation of the scheme, the evils which are dreaded and foreseen might be mitigated and avoided.'

Sir James Stephen lived for a time at Stowey House on the south side of Clapham Common. As legal adviser to the Colonial Office he was called on to draft the Bill for the Abolition of Slavery in 1833. It had been delayed by many causes, and he had to draft its sixty-six clauses between Saturday afternoon and the middle of Monday.

He became Professor of Modern History at Cambridge in 1849. The post had been pressed on Macaulay by Prince Albert, and when he declined it the chair was offered to his friend, Sir James.

Charlotte Elliott, granddaughter of Henry Venn the elder, was born at Clapham on March 18, 1789, and lived there until her removal to Brighton in 1823. It was at her father's house in Clapham in 1822 that Cæsar Malan ventured to speak to her about personal religion. She had not thought deeply about spiritual things, but his faithful words led her to Christ. 'Come to Him just as you are,' was his counsel. Her great hymn, 'Just as I am,' based on the words which had helped her to find rest, was written at Brighton in 1834.

The title 'The Clapham Sect' appears to have originated with Sydney Smith, who used it to describe the band of friends who stood shoulder to shoulder in the long fight against ignorance and oppression. The name, as Canon Overton says, is 'a little misleading. They did not " follow " any one in religion except their own parish priest, whom their leader in works of piety and charity, William Wilberforce, always consulted.' They availed themselves of every means to win their victory. 'Bibles, schools, missionaries, the circulation of evangelical books and the training of evangelical missionaries, the possession of well-attended pulpits, war through the press, and war in Parliament, against every form of injustice which either law or custom sanctioned—such were the forces by which they hoped to extend the kingdom of light and to resist the tyranny with which the earth was threatened.'

They spared neither time nor fortune in this holy war. At first they had full measure of reproach and contempt wrung out to them. When Simeon went to record his vote at the University the dons and students formed a double line and hissed him as he retired from the room. The shock was so great that Simeon broke down and stole into a neighbouring church utterly disheartened and crushed. Years brought a glorious revenge. He descended to the grave 'amidst the tears and benedictions of the poor ; and with such testimonies of esteem and attachment from the learned as Cambridge had never before rendered even to the most illustrious of her sons ; and there he was laid in that sure and certain hope on which he enabled an almost countless multitude to repose, amidst the wreck of this world's promises, and in the grasp of their last and most dreaded enemy.'

The young people at Clapham were kept in touch with the most influential religious leaders of the time. We have seen how Henry Martyn was brought on the Common by Mr. Charles Grant. There is a strain of loving hero-worship in the epitaph which Macaulay wrote in his thirteenth year. The spirit of the Clapham Sect had already fired the boy's imagination and stirred his heart.

> Here Martyn lies. In manhood's early bloom
> The Christian hero finds a pagan tomb.
> Religion, sorrowing o'er her noblest son,
> Points to the glorious trophies that he won ;
> Eternal trophies not with carnage red,
> Not stained with blood by hostile warriors shed,

But trophies of the Cross; for that dear name,
Through every form of danger, death, and shame
Onward he journeyed to a happier shore,
Where danger, death, and shame assault no more.

Another missionary hero whom the young folk knew well was Reginald Heber, who often visited Battersea Rise. Young Pennington, who lived two doors nearer London than the Macaulays, noticed one Sunday in 1826 that the Thorntons were in tears during service in Clapham Church. He was told that news had just arrived of Heber's death at Trichinopoly on April 2, 1826. Goldwin Smith often stayed with the Penningtons as a boy.

When Sir James Stephen's article on *The Clapham Sect* appeared in 1843, Macaulay wrote to one of his sisters : ' I think Stephen's article on *The Clapham Sect* the best thing he ever did. I do not think with you that the Claphamites were men too obscure for such delineation. The truth is, that from that little knot of men emanated all the Bible societies, and almost all the missionary societies, in the world. The whole organization of the Evangelical party was their work. The share which they had in providing means for the education of the people was great. They were really the destroyers of the slave trade and slavery. Many of those whom Stephen describes were public men of the greatest weight. Lord Teignmouth governed India at Calcutta ; Grant governed India in Leadenhall Street. Stephen's father was Perceval's right-hand man in the House of Commons.'

CHAPTER VII

A PILGRIMAGE IN CLAPHAM

'Clapham is supposed to have received its appellation from one of its ancient proprietors, Osgod Clapa being the name of the Danish lord at whose daughter's marriage feast Hardicanute died.' In the Chertsey Register, however, it is named Clappenham as far back as the reign of Alfred. In the Domesday Survey it is entered as Clopeham. Hughson, in his *History of London* (1808) describes Clapham as a village about four miles from Westminster Bridge, with ' many handsome houses, surrounding a Common that commands many pleasant views.' Hughson says that the Common had been little better than a morass at the beginning of the reign of George the Third, and the roads almost impassable. Largely through the exertions of Mr. Christopher Baldwin, J.P., an old resident, a public subscription was raised, the roads repaired, and ' the Common so beautifully planted with trees, that it has the appearance of a park.'

Old and New London, vi. 320.

CHAPTER VII

A PILGRIMAGE IN CLAPHAM

A VISIT to the homes and haunts of the Clapham philanthropists adds sensibly to the interest of a study of their lives and work. The best place to begin the pilgrimage is at the Notre Dame Convent School on the south side of the Common. The electric cars from London pass it a moment or two after they have left the Plough at Clapham. Two red-brick houses are joined into one block. In the house nearer Balham John Thornton was born in 1720 (p. 40). His father lived here, and his son succeeded to the estate. Such men as Henry Venn, John Newton, and the Evangelical leaders of the time were constant visitors at this house. What a story these walls could tell of John Thornton's princely generosity and simple devotion ! He made the fame of Clapham when he offered Wilberforce a room in his house (pp. 98–9), where the popular young member of Parliament might find rest and Christian converse in the country. That invitation brought its blessing to his own son Henry, who found in Wilberforce a kindred spirit and was soon fully launched on his own course of philanthropic service. After John Thornton's death Henry Venn spent a Sunday here with the bereaved family, and spoke at the old house about the friend whom he had known and loved for thirty-six years (p. 72).

After their father's death Samuel Thornton lived in this house, whilst his brother Robert occupied that on the left-hand side (pp. 174–5).

On his return from his Governor-General-ship in India, Lord Teignmouth, first President of the British and Foreign Bible Society, took the house in which John Thornton had lived. Visitors found their way to him from all parts of the world (p. 172). The traditions of the house were well maintained by Lord Teignmouth (p. 173), who was very reluctant to leave a place where he 'enjoyed all the comforts this world can afford, during seven years.' Mr. Perceval, then Chancellor of the Exchequer, spent the summer and autumn of 1807 in this old house.

Sir James Stephen (p. 221), lived at Stowey House, a few doors to the right. His father was one of Wilberforce's strongest supporters in the struggle against the slave trade; and Sir James Stephen's noble article on 'The Clapham Sect' is one of their enduring memorials. A few minutes' walk nearer Balham, just beyond Cavendish Road, stood till 1906 the splendid house of Henry Cavendish, the great chemist (p. 181), who here weighed the earth. He died in 1810.

The chief centre of the activities of the Clapham Sect was Battersea Rise House, which lies at the Wandsworth end of Clapham Common, with a narrow strip of the Common lying between it and the great thoroughfare to Clapham Junction. It was once the home of Mr. Lubbock, the banker (p. 113), and of Single-speech Hamilton; but since 1792 it has been the property of the Thornton family. When Henry Thornton and William Wilberforce lived here as bachelors, Hannah More was one of their honoured guests. The lofty oval library was built from a design suggested by William Pitt. At Battersea Rise anti-slavery plans were matured, and the delightful social gatherings of the Sect were held (p. 126). John Venn came here to consult his lay colleagues about their missionary projects. Charles Simeon was present, greatly in earnest about the spread of the gospel (p. 161). Sir Robert Inglis made the house a resort of all the men of note and genius of his day. Southey and Sir Walter Scott both visited him here (p. 215).

Glenelg, on the right-hand side, was the home of Mr. Charles Grant, the great Indian Director, and his distinguished sons, the elder of whom was Chief Secretary for Ireland, and the younger Governor of

Bombay and author of 'O worship the King,' and other hymns dear to all churches (pp. 120, 194–5). The Rev. William Arthur, the well-known Methodist President, author of *The Tongue of Fire*, and other works, lived here. At Maisonette, which stands to the east of Battersea Rise House, lived the great jurist, Sir James Mackintosh, to whom we owe that softening of our criminal law which saved sheep-stealers and forgers from the gallows (p. 181).

Broomfield, the house of Pitt's sister, and her husband, the Hon. E. Eliot, and afterwards of Wilberforce, was pulled down in 1904. It lay some distance behind Battersea Rise House, in what is now Wroughton Road. Sir Charles Forbes, who lived here from 1851 to 1877, changed the name to Broomwood (p. 121). Wilberforce published his *Practical View* the same year that he entered on possession of Broomfield. There he heard that it had led to the conversion of Legh Richmond, and there his son Samuel, afterwards Bishop of Winchester, was born (pp. 122–3).

Our pilgrimage now leads us back towards the parish church. As we pass along the north side of the Common, The Terrace, between Victoria Road and The Chase, marks the spot where once stood the house in which Samuel Pepys spent his last days, and where he was visited by John Evelyn (pp. 32–3). The house on the west side of The Chase, now 'The Hostel of God,' was the home of Sir Charles Barry, the architect of the Houses of Parliament, and in that on the east side lived Mr. Grover, the local historian, who regarded it as the oldest house on Clapham Common. A few yards eastwards we reach Church Buildings, a row of houses erected 1713–20, which are ascribed to Wren. The house on the western side of the archway nearest to Old Clapham, where Granville Sharp once lived, was the school of William Greaves, who was brought to Clapham to teach the negro boys who came from Sierra Leone with Zachary Macaulay. The Yorkshire-man afterwards attained celebrity as the first schoolmaster of Thomas Babington

THE OLD PARISH CHURCH, CLAPHAM.

Macaulay, the second Lord Teignmouth, Samuel Wilberforce, and other children of the Clapham Sect (pp. 136, 201). Clarence House, a few doors to the left, was Mr. Stroud's school, where Tom Hood was a pupil.

Their parish church filled a large place in the history of the Clapham Sect. We may first pass through the Old Town and Rectory Grove to St. Paul's Church. This stands on the site of St. Mary's, which was the parish church of Clapham till 1776. Here Henry Venn served as curate. On the north side of its graveyard John Thornton and many of his descendants rest. His great square tomb behind the church records also the names of Henry Thornton and his wife. There is a slab on the wall of the church close by in memory of Henry Thornton's daughter Marianne (pp. 216-17). The old rectory where John Venn lived was in Larkhall Lane, near the old parish church (p. 89). Grove House, the home of Charlotte Elliott's girlhood, was not far from the old rectory. Both seem to have been pulled down about 1884.

The present parish church, dedicated to the Holy Trinity, was opened in 1776, when the population of Clapham was growing rapidly (pp. 78–9). It is ninety feet long and sixty wide, so that it marked a notable advance on its modest predecessor. The spacious church, with a gallery that surrounds three sides of the building, remains much as it was in the days of William Wilberforce, though the chancel was added in 1902. The families of the famous philanthropists of Clapham worshipped here (p. 188).

At the east end of the gallery is a marble column in memory of John Thornton, who contributed largely to the erection of the building. This monument was erected in 1816 by his son, Samuel Thornton, one of the members of Parliament for Surrey.

A memorial to the rector, William Dealtry, D.D. (1813–1847), is on the north side of the gallery. The copious inscription was written by John Thornton, Jun.

Below the gallery on the north side is John Venn's marble monument, with a brass beneath it to Marianne Thornton, 1797–1887. 'She opened her mouth with wisdom.'

On the south side is the memorial of John Jebb, 'the learned, the wise, the good, Bishop of Limerick.' He died on December 9, 1833, and was buried in the tomb of the Thorntons. Nearer the chancel is the marble monument of John Thornton, Jun., Treasurer of the Church Missionary Society and the Bible Society, who died October 29, 1861, in his seventy-eighth year. He was the son of Samuel Thornton.

Nor must we overlook the neighbouring brass of John William Grover, F.S.A., the local historian, son of a former rector of Hitcham, Bucks. He died on August 23, 1892, aged fifty-six.

The parish church at Clapham is full of life, and the present rector, Canon C. P. Greene, is President of the local branch of the British and Foreign Bible Society, and well maintains that friendliness for workers of other religious communions which the Clapham Sect always cultivated.

The last step of our pilgrimage brings us to the shop, No. 5 The Pavement, which bears the name Macaulay House. It is a few doors from the Plough Inn. The tiny garden of the front has long been built over, but the house remains. Here Lord Macaulay spent his wonderful childhood (p. 199), and set out with his mother and sister on his rambles over the Common, which was a realm of unfailing romance to the gifted boy.

The pilgrimage makes an easy afternoon walk, but it will furnish material for much delightful study of the Sect which roused England to wash her hands of all complicity in the slave trade, and by its devotion to the Church Missionary Society and the Bible Society has done much to hasten the coming of that new earth wherein dwelleth righteousness.

If the visitor who has made his pilgrimage will step on board the electric car for Westminster and find his way to the Abbey, he will see Wilberforce's statue in the north aisle of the choir. Zachary Macaulay's monument is in the nave, and not far from it is that to Sir James Mackintosh. Lord Macaulay is buried in Poets' Corner. Granville Sharp's monument by Chantry is also in the south transept, and was erected by the African Society as a mark of gratitude for the labours of that noble champion of the slave. Such memorials bear witness to England's grateful remembrance of names that will always be loved and honoured in Clapham.

INDEX

Printed by Hazell, Watson & Viney Ld., London and Aylesbury.

CPSIA information can be obtained at www.ICGtesting.com
Printed in the USA
BVOW06s1244130214

344843BV00010B/273/P